Parei

Parenting

A Handbook for Parents
in association with The Gay Byrne Show

Maureen Gaffney
Andy Conway
Paul Andrews SJ
Frances Fitzgerald

Town House

Published in 1991 by
Town House
41 Marlborough Road
Donnybrook
Dublin 4

British Library Cataloguing in Publication Data available

ISBN: 0 – 948524 – 20 – 0

Acknowledgement
Fr Paul Andrews would like to acknowledge the inclusion in his material of sentences from Penelope Leach's superb *The Parents' A to Z* (Penguin: London, 1983); and of sentences and a diagram from *Parents and Teenagers* (The Open University: London, 1982).

Managing editor: Treasa Coady
Text editor: Jonathan Williams
Text and cover design: Steven Hope
Cover photographs: Barry Mason
Typeset by Printset & Design Ltd, Dublin
Printed in England by Clays Ltd

Contents

Notes on the authors

Maureen Gaffney
Maureen Gaffney qualified in Psychology at University College Cork, and received her post-graduate training at the University of Chicago. She is a Senior Clinical Psychologist in the Eastern Health Board and Research Associate in Trinity College Dublin. She was appointed a Law Reform Commissioner in 1986. She presented the RTE television series *The ABC of Pregnancy, The ABC of Parenthood* and *In Good Faith*. She is a regular contributor to many radio and television programmes on psychological matters and has written for *The Irish Independent* and other newspapers. She is married and has two children.

Andrew Conway, MA
Employed as Senior Clinical Psychologist at the Department of Child and Family Psychiatry in the Mater Misericordial Hospital, Dublin. Is senior tutor to post-graduate students of Clinical Psychology from University College Dublin. Board member of the Mater Hospital special school. Provides psychological service to Oberstown House remand and amusement centre for teenage girls, in Lusk, Co. Dublin. Married, and with his wife Breda is involved in the rearing of three children.

Paul Andrews, MA, M Psych Sc, PhD
Born Omagh, County Tyrone, 1927. Survived six schools in England and Ireland: was educated in one of them. As a Jesuit since 1944 he has been a student, teacher, headmaster, and (currently) Director of St Declan's School and Child Guidance Centre. He chaired the ICE Committee (1970–74) which reported to the Irish Government on the planning of public examinations. Works now as a psychotherapist, university lecturer and Director of St Declan's.

Frances Fitzgerald
Frances Fitzgerald graduated in Social Science from UCD, and completed her post-graduate studies in social work in the London School of Economics. She has specialised in working with children and families. She worked as a Senior Social Worker in the world-renowned Department of Child Psychiatry in the Maudsley Hospital in London. She is now a Social Worker in the Department of Child and Family Psychiatry in the Mater Hospital, Dublin. She is on the Boards of the Dublin Institute of Adult Education and the Employment Equality Agency, and is chairwoman of the Council for the Status of Women. She has three children.

Introduction

This book will be helpful to anyone who has had no training to be a parent. It is not a bible of 'dos' and 'don'ts'. Its authors' aim is not to hand down rules or edicts, but to encourage and advise you as you try to sort out the bewildering list of issues which face you and your children every day in modern Ireland.

Although children figure largely in the text, the emphasis is firmly on you, the parent, and on the *regular* problems that may confront you and your children. The authors do not deal with the very serious problems of severe child depression, suicide, sexual abuse, family violence and the like, as in these circumstances one-to-one professional advice is often needed. Instead, the authors concentrate on the everyday issues that cause disappointment, confusion and intolerance in many modern households.

Time was when life was simpler, or so it seemed: Mammy and Daddy and children, school and church. Now Irish children are reared in a variety of domestic arrangements and subjected to conflicting outside pressures which would have been unheard of even twenty years ago. Although basic values may not have changed all that much, the demands which are made today, not only by you, but on and by your children, add greatly to the tension and stress experienced by a large number of families.

The authors of *Parenting: A Handbook for Parents* give their individual views and want to help you to believe in yourself when, as often happens, you feel overwhelmed by the task of bringing children safely from babyhood to independence. The sympathetic insights into the normal ongoing development of children and parents will, they hope, encourage you to look again at the issues that get in the way of the feelings of tenderness and love. You may not agree with everything they write, but it is hoped that their thought-provoking material will bolster your own instincts and will prompt further discussion over garden walls, on school runs and on doorsteps, at parent–teacher meetings — even in pubs and coffee-shops.

The good news is that although sometimes you may feel it, you are not alone.

The first five years

Maureen Gaffney

To avoid awkward references to
he/she or him/her, I refer to girl
babies in the section on 'The first
year', to boy babies in 'The
second year' and to girls again in
'The pre-school years'.

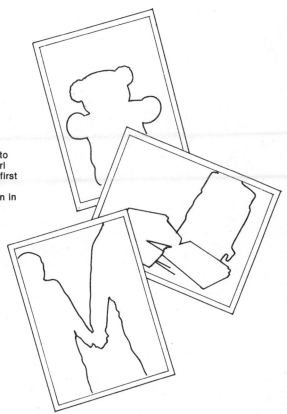

Introduction

It can safely be said that most of us who become parents do not know quite what we are letting ourselves in for. Here you are, led all your life to believe that parenting is normal, natural and right, that women have maternal instincts and that you will know what to do when you have children of your own. It will be all right on the night, you are assured.

So why are you here at two o'clock in the morning, demented from lack of sleep, frazzled by a crying baby, anxiously trying to decide whether it's a wind-pain, hunger, loneliness, downright boldness or a fatal sickness? Should you have fed him later? Not given him the baby rice? Put him to bed earlier? Not had a fight with your mother in front of him? Not given in to him last time? Or should you ring the children's hospital?

It is hardly surprising that the majority of us experience becoming a parent for the first time as a moderate to severe crisis. Learning to take care of your baby physically comes easily enough, even though initially it may be nerve-wracking. All of us eventually learn how to change a nappy and untangle an all-in-one suit. What overwhelms us is the sheer exhaustion, the relentless demands, the constant pressure on time; and, worst of all, the worry when our children are ill. Time to sleep, to relax, to have sex, to talk, even time to go to the bathroom, is in short supply. The amount of time wives and husbands spend talking to each other is reduced by as much as 50 per cent after the first child arrives. For the growing number of parents rearing children on their own, these pressures are doubled.

Then, just when you think you have mastered it all, when

11

you have proudly worked out a whole baby routine, everything changes again. When you have finally learned the delicate art of rocking your child to sleep, singing a lullaby while simultaneously managing to catnap, you suddenly find yourself having to cope with toddler temper-tantrums in the supermarket. For a while it may seem that, once again, you have an entirely new child on your hands — and that you know precisely nothing about child-rearing.

At each stage of a child's development, there are new tasks to be done, new roles to be learned — by both child and adult. There is no simple recipe for success. No matter what aspect of child-rearing you think of — discipline, aggression, showing affection, independence — questions keep cropping up. Is it too much? Too little? Too early? Too late?

Of course, this is all compensated for by the joy and pleasure children bring — the innocence, the challenge, the affection, the chance to watch a new life unfold, both reflecting your own life and ploughing its own unique furrow; and for parents themselves, the second chance it often gives to undo their own less than happy experience of being a child, the chance to do it better. These experiences make for bonds of love that run very deep indeed.

The hand that rocks the cradle

If child-rearing is meant to be instinctive, how is it that so many parents feel unsure about how to bring up their own children? One important reason is that modern parents, particularly mothers, labour under the impression that if they are sufficiently competent they can rear superior children — and that any less-than-superior children have their mother to blame. They feel they must be perfect mothers and their children must have perfect lives.

This is a tall order in a society like ours, where there is less emphasis on traditional child-rearing practices, where there is no prevailing view about the right way to rear children, and where there is nobody to teach you how to do the job — unless, of course, you have already failed.

Is it any wonder that most mothers feel anxious about their children and responsible for how they turn out? That at some stage, almost every mother ends up hating herself and feeling abnormal? That mothers who spend a lot of time with young children feel guilty because at times they become impatient and angry? And that when they spend less time with their children, they feel guilty about that too?

It seems that the standards of excellence for mothering are so high that you cannot win. Although mothers, by and large, love their children, motherhood very often drives them up the wall — at least that brand of exclusive, round-the-clock mothering that we have institutionalised.

Traditional versus modern child-rearing

Traditionally, it was success enough actually to rear a child to adulthood. So many children died, that merely to ensure a child's physical survival was a full-time job. Our parents knew little about child psychology. They thought children 'grew out of things', that they were not affected by events like death or separations from their families because they were 'too young to understand'.

But in those days society was more stable, more religious. Things did not change so quickly. People had few opportunities to alter their station in life or even their lifestyle. To rear a child who was decent, respectable and could adjust to his or her place in society was a common aim. Parents knew, or thought they knew, the world they were preparing their children for.

But we are living today in that cliché, a rapidly changing world. Think, for example, of how contraception has changed the nature of family life. We can choose (within limits) how many children to have and when to have them. More important, the age-old link between having sex and having babies has been broken. This has had profound consequences for the role of women, for accepted sexual morality, for sexual behaviour. In barely one generation, couples living together and single parenthood have become tolerated, if not universally accepted.

This continuous, even quickening, pace of change is what we mean when we talk about the stress of modern life. We cannot foresee where it will all end. The pressure this puts on parents is enormous. Their job is to prepare their offspring for a world that even they cannot foresee.

We cannot sit our children on our knees and say 'Watch what

I do; follow me'. Instead, we have to prepare them for anything, literally. We have to make sure that they are generally competent and steady — yet ready for novelty, ready to adapt. We try to give them the skills that can be applied to any new problem: judgement, reasoning, creativity. We try to teach them to be self-confident, ready to take risks, not to be afraid of challenge; to be persistent and optimistic in the face of failure. In other words, we try to rear children with high self-esteem, who feel that opportunity is there to be grasped and that they have as good a chance as anybody else of succeeding. To be confident, they have to be secure; to be secure, they have to be loved and content.

That is the job, the blueprint, that modern parents are handed. Not in so many words, of course, not explicitly. Nobody remembers where they picked up the idea; but pick it up they did. Nowadays the stakes are high in child-rearing. The great irony is that, despite all this, some of us still cling to the idea that all we need in the way of preparation is whatever kind of rearing we got ourselves.

Enter the experts . . .

Some parents grow impatient when there are not ready answers. They become anxious and cynical about the changing fads and fashions in child-rearing. There always seems to be an expert who is ready to rush to the rescue with a brand new formula. But the truth is that there is no secret formula, no magic ingredient (except maybe love), no single recipe that makes it easy to be a parent.

Child psychology does not have all the answers either, but it does have something to offer parents. Scientific child psychology has accumulated a body of information that does throw light on many aspects of child-rearing. In particular, it has helped to identify certain patterns of parenting that usually have negative consequences and others that have happier outcomes for both children and their parents.

The trouble is that the best information is not always available to those who need it most — the parents. It is perfectly sensible for modern parents to want to know just as much about child psychology and parenting as they want to know about sterilising bottles, the Three-in-One vaccine or the latest on allergies and food additives. They may not want all the technical details, but they do want to feel generally informed on the subject, to know enough to make good decisions.

That is my purpose here. The idea is not to raise anxieties for you as a parent, but to help you feel confident that you can work out solutions for yourself. Because you can. My aim will be to get you to reflect on how things look from your child's angle; to help you become more aware of your own reactions and why you respond as you do; and to build on your own good instincts and insights about your child.

Fathers and mothers

Parents means mothers *and* fathers, not mothers alone. It is a fact, of course, that mothers take responsibility for nearly all the day-to-day care of children and that most of the research is on mother-child interaction. But it is also true that fathers have a very significant role to play in rearing their children, above and beyond being good providers. Thus, everything I have to say here is addressed to both parents, unless the context specifically indicates otherwise. Of course, an increasing number of parents rear their children alone, without partners; yet, although parenting may be more stressful in those circumstances, the basic issues are very much the same.

In the days when a woman's status came from her skill in child-rearing, it suited everybody to talk about 'maternal instinct'. We now know that fathers can care for their babies just as sensitively as mothers. In particular, fathers often play in a very skilled way with even the youngest infants and are just as adept as mothers in speaking 'baby talk'. The attachment between fathers and their infants can be very strong and its quality is affected by many things. His presence at the birth helps the initial bonding with the infant, and the stronger his relationship with the mother, the better his bond with the baby. It is a finely balanced set of relationships. Each parent is dependent on the other to be as good a parent as he or she can be. The baby is dependent on both.

As well as the direct influence fathers have on their children, they also have a crucial role in making good *mothering* possible. To see why this is so, think for a moment about what mothers do. Mothering, above all else, is about responding to children's needs so that they can psychologically function to the best of their ability. Women's strength is that they are so good, almost too good, at responding to others' needs. Fathers are critical, then, not just for rescuing mothers from the ropes after the sixth round with the kids, but also as confidants and advisors. Fathers can help mothers to give themselves permission to attend directly to their own needs and to set sensible limits on responding to others.

Even women who are battling against great personal odds, who are coping with low self-esteem and depression (often the legacy of their own unhappy childhoods), can still become very successful mothers if they have a supportive partner. Unfortunately, it is equally clear that when it comes to child-rearing, a partner who is not supportive is worse than no partner at all. Single mothers, for example, are rather less likely to abuse their children than are couples.

Long-term and short-term goals

The everyday demands of children are so great that it is all too easy just to keep responding to them in a short-term way and to forget the long-term goal. From the very beginning, then, the first question you must ask yourself is: what kind of teenager do I want to rear and for what kind of world? Given the pace at which our world is changing, none of us really knows what challenges our children may face.

Since we cannot prepare them for definite tasks or specific future lives, we must help them instead to develop general coping skills and personal values. For example, we must help them to be thoughtful as opposed to impulsive, to be competent, flexible, ready to face challenges and not afraid to take risks, but at the same time to be appropriately cautious, and caring of their own and others' welfare. We can encourage them not to be passive and defeatist in the face of challenge or failure, but instead to be confident and to have high self-esteem; to feel that opportunity is there to be grasped and that they are capable of seizing it; to have a strong sense of values and, particularly in adolescence, to be able to resist temptation and remain true to their better selves.

The next question to ask, no matter how young your child is now, is how can I promote these goals at *this particular stage* of my child's development? Very often parents' short-term and long-term goals will be in conflict. At a very simple level, the parent in the short-term, i.e. right now, may want peace and quiet. Demanding immediate and unquestioning obedience may achieve that goal. The problem is that this style of rearing, while achieving our short-term goal, may endanger our more important long-term goal. For example, do we want to produce an adult whose most ready response to emotional pressure and confrontation is to submit?

Even when you are clear about long-term goals, however, another question looms: can you achieve with any certainty the outcome you desire for your children? Unless you want to drive yourself crazy, perhaps the best answer is a qualified 'yes'. As parents, we cannot control our children's destiny. Children come into this world with different capacities and different temperaments. Parents are not the only influence on a child's life. The larger family, schools, society at large are also shaping the child. This may be stating the obvious, but it is surprising how many parents behave with their children as if it is not.

Most helpful of all, perhaps, is to abandon the notion of being a perfect, or an all-powerful, parent, and instead aim to be a good parent. The aim of a good parent is not perfection, but rather to find a way to cope that best suits the situations in which you and your child will find yourselves. Instead of restricting yourself to thinking in terms of 'right' versus 'wrong', try instead to find better rather than worse ways of dealing with the challenges of rearing your child.

Children can let us know very effectively what they want and need. The trick is for parents to learn to observe, listen and talk to their children.

Nobody will ever need you as much as your children do. Nobody will ever take you as seriously, or be more influenced by you, than your children. Realising this fact can make us feel giddy with power, elation and anxiety in about equal measure. It is precisely that rush of feelings and adrenalin that gives us the courage and energy to bring a unique individual into the world and to keep pace with the day-by-day, minute-by-minute challenges of bringing up a child.

The first year

The growth of attachment

Your baby arrives like the proverbial visitor from Mars. She does not know the language, she has no idea what is required of her, and she is helpless in the ways of this world. Until the moment of your baby's delivery into this strange environment, everything she needed was provided automatically in her mother's womb: food, elimination of waste products, warmth, protection, comfort and company. Now her own little body has to learn to do all this for itself. Because of her physical helplessness, of course, somebody has to help her. She could not survive on her own.

The only handle your baby has on this bewildering place is you, her major caretaker. If she can successfully communicate her needs to you, and you meet these needs, she will survive. But you also have to be her travel-guide in exploring and joining the rest of human society. As her mother, you physically brought her into the world. As a parent — mother, father, biological or adoptive — you now have to assist in her psychological birth, her development into the unique person she was meant to be.

This is a daunting task. Like most parents, you want your child to grow up happy, competent, eager to learn and enjoy herself, able to get on well with people and to use her unique talents. But you probably also feel that you have more than enough to do just taking care of her needs at the moment. However, the two tasks are not separate. Your day-to-day caretaking is the actual means by which you develop a relationship with your baby. The way you look after your baby has profound consequences for the way she will grow as a person. Just *taking* care of her will ensure her physical survival; *how* you take care of her will determine her psychological well-being.

If, in the first vital year, she can communicate her needs to you and you respond generously, sensitively and consistently, she will trust you and feel that the world is a manageable place. For all her helplessness, if she has a sense of control over her small world through you, she will feel the same about the larger world later. That early feeling of power and control is the very foundation of her self-esteem and ability to cope.

Sensitive caretaking can happen only if she and you form a strong, secure attachment. That is the major task of her first year. Attachment means love, of course, but it means a lot more. As in an adult love relationship, love and security can flourish between a parent and child only if they can communicate well with each other. Good parenting, then, requires accurately noticing, interpreting and responding to a baby's signals. To be a good parent you must be a good communicator.

For about the first six months of your baby's life, her relationship with you has a very special quality. She does not yet know where she ends and you begin; she has hardly any awareness that her body is hers, and not yours. When her hands or her toes appear in her field of vision, she 'discovers' them; when they disappear from view, she 'loses' them. In the same way, you are real to her only when she can 'sense' you, by seeing, hearing, smelling and feeling you.

Just as she cannot separate her body from yours, she cannot separate her needs from the way you respond to these needs. Her hunger and your feeding her become part of 'her'. If you care for her well, you become her 'other half'. If you respond to her in a way that is confident, competent, loving and secure, your way of doing this becomes part of her self. She begins to feel confident, competent, loving and secure. It is that quality that makes her attachment to you so special. She sees you as part of her. What you do will become part of her.

Of course, she will develop other passionate relationships — with her father, with a brother or sister, with other family members. By eighteen months, she will have developed strong attachments to at least three people. These relationships may have a different quality from that with her major caretaker (usually her mother) but they are very important for her.

However, your baby will still have a preferred attachment figure — the person she turns to when she is under stress, tired or ill; the person whose presence makes her feel secure and whose absence distresses her and causes her to protest. This is usually, though not always, her mother. The critical factor is not 'maternal instinct'. It is simply that her major caretaker has become intimately familiar with her ways, and can be relied on to behave and respond in a predictable fashion when she is needed.

Types of attachment in babies

Most mothers form secure attachments with their babies. Studies suggest that by age one, about two-thirds of babies are securely attached. The remaining one-third are insecurely attached. Using a technique called 'the strange situation', psychologists have been able to identify three different types of attachment in one-year-old babies. A baby and mother are brought into a comfortable room with lots of toys. A stranger enters and sits talking to the mother and to the baby. The mother then leaves the room for about three minutes. Later she returns. This happens twice. The first time she leaves the baby with the stranger, the second time she leaves the baby alone. The reunion of child and mother are observed by a psychologist through a one-way mirror.

Most infants behave in the way you might expect (Type B below). In this kind of reaction, a baby who has been distressed by the separation immediately approaches her mother and tries to make physical contact with her. If the baby has not been distressed, she greets her mother when she returns and tries to make contact with her. But other infants behaved in a different way (Type A and C below), resembling the reaction of infants who have endured longer, more traumatic separations from their parents.

The three patterns of child behaviour have been described as follows:

Type A: Avoidant
Before the mother's separation, the baby plays with the toys. She is not unduly distressed by the mother's leaving and is easily

comforted by the stranger. At the reunion, the baby usually ignores the mother, or she may approach the mother tentatively, looking away or turning away as she approaches her. The infant may pick up, or hang on to, an object — as if to distract herself — but will not play with it. She may look blankly at the mother, but will show no open fear or distress and, most important, no anger. If the mother picks up her baby, the baby may show that she wants to be put down. The infant will not indicate this in an emotional way by struggling or protesting, but in a subtle way, by bending towards the floor or pointing to an object — as if to distract the mother's attention. The infant may be more friendly to the stranger than to the mother.

Type B: Secure
Before the separation, the baby will play with the toys and explore the room. She may or may not become distressed when the mother leaves. If she is distressed, however, she will cry or will stop or reduce her playing. When the mother returns, the baby will go to her immediately, seeking contact. If she was distressed by the separation, she may greet the mother with an outraged cry and usually will settle for nothing less than being held. She calms down while she is being held and then resumes play. The baby shows no avoidance of the mother or resistance to her.

Type C: Resistant
Before the separation, the baby may be fussy and wary, keeping an eye on her mother's whereabouts. She may be distressed even before the first separation, fearful of the stranger and extremely distressed by the separation itself. Upon reunion, the baby will go to the mother and seek contact with her, but at the same time will resist it by struggling to get down and may get angry. The baby will not readily resume play and will remain preoccupied with the mother, just as she was before the separation.

Both 'avoidant' and 'resistant' behaviour indicate an insecure attachment. As a child approaches one year of age, the kind of attachment she has to her major caretaker is a reliable indicator of how happily she will play in her second year, how well she will form relationships with other people, and how co-operative she will be. The quality of her attachment will determine how competently she will strive to solve problems, whether she knows when to ask for help and when to do things for herself, and how persistent she will be in completing tasks.

The effects go on. By age three-and-a-half, the type of early attachment the child had to the mother will influence how self-directed she is and how well she is able to amuse herself. It also will affect how curious she is about the world around her, how socially competent or withdrawn she is, how well able she is to respond to the distress of another person, and whether other children seek out her company. By age five, the kind of early attachment she had with her mother influences how flexibly she copes with change. The type of attachments formed in the early years can persist right into adult life, affecting how we cope with stress, what kind of love relationships we form, and how we behave as parents.

Being insecurely attached weakens a child psychologically, makes her vulnerable to stress and makes it more likely that she will repeat unhappy patterns in subsequent relationships. This is not to say that things we learn early in life solely decide our subsequent happiness and success; that patterns laid down in the first years cannot be changed. On the contrary, at any stage of parenting it is possible to modify your relationship and to try other, more helpful ways of communicating with your child. As a parent you are not stuck with just one way of doing things. If you feel you are, you have only to ask yourself 'who says?'

The three patterns of attachment are associated with different styles of caretaking. For example, children with an avoidant pattern (Type A) often have mothers who strongly dislike physical contact with them, who speak mockingly and sarcastically about them and who care for them in a stiff, emotionless way. The mothers do show frequent anger, yet will react in a detached way to the child's attempts to make contact with them; for example, they will show no change of expression even when the child physically attacks them. Children with a resistant pattern of attachment (Type C) have mothers who do not reject their children, but are very insensitive and inconsistent in the way they care for them. Though they may be sometimes warm and co-operative, they are unpredictable and the child has little confidence that her needs will be met. Children with a secure pattern of attachment (Type B) have mothers who are sensitive and responsive to their children's needs.

The importance of responsiveness

The key word for effective parenting in the first year is 'responsiveness'. The more responsive you are, the more securely attached your baby will be at the end of her first year. You may be lucky. This approach may come naturally to you, but most of us can become more skilled as parents. Your best teacher will be your own baby. Your most important task as a new parent is to notice how she reacts to things. Watch her, listen to her, wait for her reactions; allow her the time to communicate with you. Your baby has likes and dislikes, good moods and bad moods, just like anybody else. Responsiveness means taking care of your baby's needs in a way that is *sensitive, accepting, co-operative* and *accessible*. Here are some guidelines.

Being sensitive to your baby's signals

● Learn her language by learning to read her signals. A baby's range of signals is very limited. She can cry, she can smile; later she can make babbling sounds. She can look closely or she can look away. She can kick and wave her arms, or she can stiffen. She can open her eyes wide or she can close them momentarily. She can frown and she can laugh. She can move towards you or pull away.

These signals may not look very impressive, but they are your baby's only way of communicating. By observing her signals you will find out what she likes and what she dislikes, what comforts her and what distresses her. Her signals will tell you when she wants more of something and when she wants less; when she is in a good mood and when she is not; when she wants company and when she wants to be left alone. She can communicate well only if you learn to recognise her signals. You can care for her sensitively only if you try to understand what she is telling you.

• If you are unsure about her signals, try responding in a particular way, all the time watching her reaction. If you are responding correctly, she will give you a cue. The important thing is to wait for her reaction before you continue or try something else.

• Try to respond to her signals (for instance, her cries of hunger) rather than to the dictates of some 'correct' schedule. The only correct schedule is the one that keeps your baby content most of the time. Of course, you will have to develop a routine, but try to do it gradually and to shape it around her natural rhythm, rather than impose it. All babies, no matter how irregular they may be at first, eventually adjust their patterns and fit in, more or less, with the family schedule. You cannot, on cue, make a baby be hungry, eat, sleep or be in a good mood.

• Try to respond to her signals rather than to your own wishes, moods or expectations. If you feel like cuddling her or playing with her because you have been out, or you feel in a good mood, think whether she may feel like it just now. Is she resting contentedly? Engrossed in a game? Give her a moment to get used to your presence, wait for a cue, which you will almost certainly get, then hug and kiss her to your heart's content.

There will be days when you are in a bad mood. You may be disinclined to react to her overtures, yet you know instinctively that it is unfair to 'take it out' on her. Some parents find themselves becoming irritable at things their baby is doing that normally would not bother them. Parents who are depressed may hold on to and hug their baby because they feel in need of comfort themselves, rather than because the baby has signalled that she needs comfort. They may ignore the baby's wriggling to get down or her attempts to communicate what she actually wants (such as to make eye-contact with the mother or to play). If this happens, the baby is getting mixed signals. She is being cuddled and ignored at the same time. Think of how you would react if you found yourself being intimately handled by somebody who was not interested in what you wanted. It is not that different for the baby.

This is a very hard situation to manage, particularly if it happens frequently. You are in need of sympathy yourself. Try to build something into the day that will keep both of you reasonably agreeable, and will not put too much pressure on you to keep your baby entertained. A long walk is a good solution. If you have a bad day only occasionally, it is not going to do her any harm, but if you find yourself so consistently under stress that you cannot respond to her signals, you need to talk to a professional who can help you.

Parents who are experiencing problems with their children often talk and play with them just as much as parents who are coping well. The difference between the two groups is that when the problem parents are affectionate or playful it is less likely to have arisen from the *child's* prompts or demands.

Try to see things from your baby's point of view. Babies have so many needs to communicate and so few ways of transmitting them. Think how you would feel yourself if you were laid low in a foreign country and you had to communicate with people who could not speak your language.

Notice what is going on inside yourself. The better you know your own reactions and the more you know about your own unbringing, the more sensitive you can be with your baby. For example, you may know that as a child you were locked into a power-struggle with your mother, and because of this you react badly to any kind of pressure to submit. If you begin to notice yourself reacting to your baby's demands by thinking 'She will not get the better of me', this may give you pause. You may think 'Who is my battle with, my baby who needs me or my mother who dominated me?' This realisation in itself will not solve your problem, but it is a first and vital step in breaking a pattern of reacting, and in overcoming past mistakes.

Unless you keep in touch with your own feelings, your reactions may distort how you interpret your baby's signals. Her tears can be misinterpreted as a sign that your baby does not love you, or as her deliberate attempt to provoke you. In extreme situations, parents who misinterpret their baby's facial expression of distress as anger at them are at risk of abusing their child.

If you find yourself reacting like this to your baby, it is not a sign that either of you is an impossible person. The more likely reason is that you are carrying over into your relationship with your baby unresolved problems from another relationship. Unless you come to some understanding of these problems and find a way of coping with them, sensitive parenting will be desperately difficult for you.

Accepting your baby for what she is

Accepting your baby for what she is may come easily to you, especially if she is the kind of baby you expected and you find her easy to understand. If she is not, you may have negative feelings towards her from time to time. It is far better to acknowledge these disappointed feelings to yourself or, better still, to discuss them with somebody you trust. Babies notice feelings in others, especially in their parents. Well-intentioned efforts to hide or disguise your feelings are likely to lead to a stiff and detached style of caretaking that will unsettle the baby and make her anxious.

Reflect on your feelings when you were in the company of somebody whom you sensed did not like you, even though they were trying to hide it. Most likely you experienced feelings of tension, uncertainty as to what you may have done wrong, worry about what you could do to put it right, or a sense that there was simply no point in trying with someone who did not like you. Because there was no open acknowledgment of the problem, there could be no solution. You probably decided to avoid that person as far as possible. That may be the only thing a baby can do in similar circumstances.

● Accepting your baby means accepting being a parent. You can help yourself to do that by setting realistic standards of good parenting. Rearing children is very hard work. It requires major adjustments in your life, especially in the first few years. Yet being a parent, particularly being a mother, does not mean that you must be an uncanonised saint and martyr, ever-patient, selfless and passively accepting. Aim rather for a feeling of cheerful resignation to the demands of parenthood. Even the most accepting parents occasionally feel irritated or driven crazy by their children.

● Practise being positive. Try to notice and enjoy your baby's good days and happy moods. In particular, spend time playing with her every day, even though initially you may feel bored or 'no good' at playing, or guilty because you are not working. Persist and you will get better. Gradually, you will begin to relax and her enjoyment will be infectious. The idea is to associate parenting with as much pleasure as possible, and to avoid situations where the baby is associated with nothing but chores.

Learning to be co-operative

● Cultivate respect for your baby. 'Respect' is not a word we normally associate with babies, but it is turning out to be an important word in research on parenting. Respect means thinking of your baby as a separate, unique person with her own will and preferences.

● Learning to be co-operative with your baby mainly means avoiding unnecessary interference with her body, her will, her activities and her preferences. When you have to do something with your baby, try to give her due warning. For example, if you have to lift her from a sleepy or relaxed state, do not suddenly pick her up. Instead, stand or kneel over where she is lying, talk to her gently for a while, stroke her face or body, if possible wait for a signal that she would like to be moved (a movement towards you, an excited waving of her hands or kicking) and then lift her. This need not take very long, but the extra few minutes will build a gentle, co-operative style into your relationship with her.

● When you want your baby to do something that she is unhappy about, such as changing her nappy or giving her a bath while she is playing contentedly, ask yourself if you have to do it right away. Waiting a bit longer until she is in the mood often will mean that the job will be done faster anyway, precisely because she is co-operating.

If you have to interrupt her, try to get her co-operation by distracting her. This is where your play time with her will come in handy, because you will be much better informed about her current favourite game.

● If you find yourself frequently opposing your baby's will, or becoming preoccupied that she is trying to get the better of you, or feeling determined that she will not get her way, it may simply be that you have not considered other ways of dealing with her. This kind of difficulty often arises when parents do not notice the child's signals. If the baby objects, there is an immediate confrontation and the mother exerts direct control.

Learning to be accessible

● The secret of being accessible to your baby is to be in good communication with her. This means being able to see and hear her signals. The best way to do this is to keep her physically near you, but even if she has moved further away, as she will towards the end of her first year, cultivate the habit of being 'tuned in' to her moods and activities.

● Respond as quickly as you can to her signals. Ignoring them will result in her learning lessons that will not be in either of your interests. If you never respond to her signals that she wants to play, be held, be comforted or talked to, she may stop asking altogether. If your baby is exceptionally resourceful, she may learn to amuse herself, but her learning will be very limited compared to what it could be with you as a teacher.

Do not be fooled into thinking that because she is 'not bothering you' she is learning to be independent. What she is learning is to be detached. One of the consequences may be that when your daughter becomes older, she will spend as much time as possible avoiding you. She may spend a lot of time away from home, and the family may not be able to exercise as much control over her activities as you would wish.

● If you delay for as long as possible in responding to your baby's signals, it teaches her a lesson that you may live to regret. If you respond only when she has intensified her signals to such an extent (for instance by howling and fussing) that she can no longer be ignored, then she will come to realise that this is the best way to get your attention. You will have taught her to be a cranky, demanding baby, and maybe a cranky, demanding teenager and adult too.

● Delaying as long as possible before responding will confuse your child's feelings. Her need for you and the pleasure she gets when you do respond will get mixed up with feelings of frustration and anger. In other words, she learns a pattern of loving somebody who is not making her happy. Or she learns a pattern of never fully loving somebody because of a fear that she will be hurt. Is this the view of love you want her to have as a young adult?

● You cannot respond all the time to your baby. Set appropriate limits so that you can get the rest and relaxation that you need to be a good parent. You will do yourself and your baby no favour if you run yourself into the ground.

Having set your limits, learn to say 'Yes' to your baby with strength and conviction, and learn to say 'No' with love. Responding readily to your baby in the first year will not result in a spoilt child. On the contrary, it will help your child to be competent, independent, socially likeable and responsive to other people's feelings in the next and subsequent years. Think of it as money in the bank. You are building up credit with your child. You can call on this credit in the second year when the child is capable of more active co-operation.

Getting to know your baby

Babies who are securely attached at the end of the first year usually have mothers who are able to report minute details about their babies' reactions and progress. Mothers who are vague about their babies' characteristics and preferences, on the other hand, tend to have babies who are insecurely attached. It makes good sense to go to some trouble to get to know your baby.

One of the fundamental ways that babies differ from each other is in temperament — the general disposition we have towards life which reveals how active, emotional and sociable we are. From birth, babies have been found to be different from each other in nine ways:

- *Activity level.* Some babies are active. They kick a lot in the womb, they wriggle and move in their cots, and as toddlers they will always run rather than walk. Other babies are much less active and stay still for longer periods.

- *Regularity.* Some babies have regular cycles of activity. They eat, sleep and excrete on schedule almost from birth. Other babies are much less predictable.

- *Approach to novelty.* Some babies revel in everything new. Others seem to dread novelty. The 'approach' baby splashes with delight in the bath, smiles at strangers and eats new foods heartily. The 'withdrawal' baby is scared of the bath, is shy with strangers and will make a face at every new food.

- *Adaptability.* Some babies adjust quickly to change while others become distressed at any change in their routine.

- *Intensity of reaction.* Some babies laugh with great spirit and bring the house down when they cry. Other babies react much less intensively; they smile when they are happy and whimper rather than cry.

- *Level of awareness.* There are babies who react to the slightest sound, sight or touch. The least thing disturbs their sleep. They will blink and turn away even from a distant light. Other babies seem unaware of even loud noise, bright lights or dirty nappies.

- *Mood.* Some babies are almost always happy, smiling and in good form. Others too often seem grouchy, miserable and complain a lot.

- *Distractibility.* Some babies are easily distracted. Playing with them or singing a song will keep their minds off their hunger, at least while you are preparing to feed them. They can be distracted from exploring the contents of your purse by giving them a set of keys. Other babies are relentlessly single-minded.

- *Attention span.* Some babies play contentedly with a toy

for a long time (by baby standards, at least). Others flit from one toy or game to another.

Many aspects of temperament seem to be largely innate, but others change as the baby gets older. Yet what is really changeable is the expression of all these characteristics. Your job as a parent is to help your baby find a better, rather than a worse, way of expressing and coping with her particular temperament.

The world has room for all sorts of personalities. Reflect, for example, on people you know who are active, sociable and also happy and successful in life. Then think of people who are equally active and sociable but who are chronically unsettled because they have never learned to channel their energies or are too easily influenced by other people.

This is not to say that all babies are easy to rear. Most (65 per cent) fall into one of three categories: easy (about 40 per cent), slow-to-warm-up (about 15 per cent) and difficult (about 10 per cent). The rest show mixed patterns, but this does not mean that babies stay in the same category as they get older. As they pass through the different phases of childhood, their moods change quite a lot.

Many problems arise not from having a baby whom *other* people might describe as 'easy' or 'difficult', but from having a baby whom *you* find difficult. Your baby may have a temperament that does not suit yours. For example, you may find it a joy to rear an active baby who loves novelty and stimulation, and who loudly expresses her wishes and reactions; or you may find it exhausting. You may be delighted with a passive, timid baby with regular habits, or you may be disappointed. Problems can also arise if you misread a baby's temperament. For example, if you do not understand that your baby is truly frightened by novelty, you may continue, with the best of intentions, to try to 'jolly' her out of her fear. It would be more helpful to concentrate on protecting her from too much novelty for the time being and to find ways of introducing novelty in small, manageable doses. The sensible thing is to adjust your style to suit your baby.

Controlling the amount of stimulation is the key — reducing it for 'slow-to-warm-up' babies, increasing it for active and curious babies. It also helps to learn to anticipate difficult

moments in the day and to try to prevent the build-up of
frustration. If you can anticipate your baby's need for comfort,
company or stimulation before she starts acting up, you have
the advantage, and you will not feel stressed and frustrated.

You may need to build in a lot of time for comforting cranky
babies, just as you would if the child had a physical ailment.
You would do this automatically if your baby made demands
because of a physical complaint. You may find yourself being
unwilling to do the same for a baby who is demanding by
nature. This may be because you think that your baby is
deliberately being difficult, and therefore that she is to blame.
Or you may fear that she is difficult because you are not a good
parent, so you are to blame. Blame has no part in this. Blaming
will demoralise you and prevent you from using your energy
and creativity to devise practical solutions. Stop fighting her
temperament. Accept that this is the way she is, at least for
the time being. Console yourself with the thought that if you
meet this challenge successfully, you will begin to feel a special
and well-earned confidence in yourself as a parent. This will
stand you in good stead in the years ahead.

Physical development in the first year

Nature provides your newborn baby with a survival kit of
reflexes. She does not have to think. All she has to do is respond
to a stimulus in a particular way. She will suck anything that
touches her lips; she will turn her head and start to suck
whenever something brushes against her cheek and she will
cry when her stomach is empty. These reflexes do not just help
her to get the nutrition she needs; they attract her parents. If
you are her mother, your baby's sucking and even her crying
releases a hormone in you which helps make your breast milk
flow — the perfect demand-and-supply system.

An infant's cry is so disturbing to most adults that they
cannot long resist it. The sense of relief when they can soothe
a crying baby is so great that most parents are programmed
to learn quickly how to respond. The baby is ready to teach
them. Being picked up, held, rocked, warmed, fed, walked
about — these will stop the crying and make the parent feel
good, competent and in control. The baby, who has succeeded
in communicating her needs to the parent and having them

met will feel the same way — good, competent and in control. Both baby and parent are thinking 'I can do it'.

But Nature also has provided your baby with other skills that make it attractive for you to take care of her. From the very beginning, she is programmed to find other humans intensely interesting. When newborn, she can focus well only on objects that are about ten inches away. This is the usual distance between you and your baby when you hold her in the crook of your arm. That bodily contact between you comforts her and makes it possible for her to study your face. She will not be able to see in the way adults do until she is about six months old, so it is important to put her toys and mobiles where she can look at them.

By two months, she will like looking at faces best of all. At three months, not only can she recognise you, but she can recognise your photograph. She can recognise and respond to your facial expressions. By four months she will have become even more expert at recognising familiar people.

Your baby can hear clearly. She will be soothed by the sound of a heartbeat, another reason for holding her often in your arms. She will turn her head in the direction of a noise and will pay even more attention to the sound of a conversation. By one month, she can distinguish her mother's voice from other female voices and prefers that voice. At that age she can distinguish very similar sounds from each other. You can observe her 'freeze' to attention or kick with excitement when she senses that you are talking to her. By four months she is able to recognise the voices of most of the people who are close to her. Again, you can observe her attention and excitement when she hears the approach of the parent who plays with her. Fathers usually play with infants in a very robust way. They move the baby's legs and arms in imitation of kicking or climbing. They zoom the baby through the air and tickle her. Mothers play in a quieter, more soothing way. Even at three months, babies notice the difference between the two approaches; they react with more visible excitement to their father's approach and are more likely to laugh and to cry while playing with their fathers.

Babies' first social response is their smile. Just as their crying is designed to galvanise adults into comforting and nurturing, their smile is designed to get adults to learn how to communicate and play with them. Most otherwise restrained adults will do anything to get an infant to smile and, once having achieved it, will keep repeating it, much to their own and the baby's satisfaction.

During her first six months, your baby will smile more and more. If you look, you will see that she smiles when she recognises something that initially had seemed strange. You will see that smile more and more as she begins to recognise you. You will find this very gratifying and will smile back and talk to her. Your baby will respond by smiling some more and using whatever sounds she can make as communication with you.

Gradually, with observation and practice, you and your baby learn the sequence of actions that produces the most smiles. To an outsider, this sequence may seem unimpressive. For example, you may make quick 'tutting' noises, may open and close your eyes and mouth in mock surprise, or raise or lower your voice. Meanwhile the baby responds by staring or looking away, widening or closing her eyes, making sounds, smiling or frowning, moving with your movements or stiffening.

But what is fascinating and psychologically very important is how the sensitive parent, familiar with the baby's ways, will adjust his or her actions to the baby's signals. Thus, the parent will intensify or repeat the sound or action when the baby smiles, keeps looking and moves with them, but will reduce or stop the action when the baby turns away or frowns. Simple as this sounds, it has been found to be the beginning of the partnership between parents and their babies on which the baby's secure attachment will be built.

In the second half of the first year your baby is beginning to move around. Crying and smiling are no longer the only ways she can keep in close contact with you. Now she can crawl after you. Her attachment to you makes her want to stay close. Her curiosity about the world makes her want to move away and explore. You now play a new role in her life. You are her secure base. She will have the confidence to move away, as long as she can keep you at a comfortable distance.

If you observe her at this stage, you will see her giving you frequent glances — ones that seem to be saying 'Look what I am doing, what do you think of that?' She will then pause, as if inviting you to say 'Oh look what you are doing! What a clever girl you are!' Being 'tuned in' to those glances, being available to look, listen, pay attention is vital. For your baby it means 'You are there for me'.

From time to time, she will continue to glance and listen to make sure that you are still there, looking, listening, paying attention. Or she will get your attention by bringing and showing you toys and objects. If she senses that you have moved further away, or that your activities have become quieter, she may call out to you, as if saying 'Is everything still OK? Are you still there?' If something alarms her, she will scuttle back to you, her haven. When this begins to happen, usually around six months of age, children have become truly attached.

How your baby learns to think

Between birth and adolescence your child's intelligence will go through a number of distinct stages. The first stage lasts until about age two, during which, unlike adults, she thinks exclusively with her senses and her body. Babies do not think about a rattler. Instead they suck, bang and shake it. That is how they 'know' it. It is an action-bound intelligence.

At first, your baby is still simply reacting to the world, but by about four months she has reached a new stage: she has become more aware of objects and people around her and has begun to recognise what they can do. Realising that rattlers make a noise, for example, babies will shake a rattler and gurgle with laughter the minute they are handed one. At this stage, your baby's intellectual drive is to try to make all these interesting new sights and sounds last and thus produce exciting experiences for herself. Your role is to be her helper in this important work. You have to provide the kinds of objects that the baby can experiment on, things on which she can produce a variety of sounds and movements, for example. Her own toys are important, but equally interesting are household objects, provided they are safe; you can give her different size saucepans, a plastic bowl and a wooden spoon so that she can experiment by producing different sounds.

Nevertheless, your baby's most important 'toy' is you. You can help her to explore the different possibilities in everything you give her, showing her how to stack boxes, put lids on saucepans, build towers; or at least you can build towers so that she can knock them down. At this stage, she will love to make sounds, listen for a response, and then answer back. If you answer her, you are amusing her, but you are also teaching her an important lesson — when someone calls, a response is required. This is what you will want her to know in a few short months when she is a toddler.

At eight months, another dramatic development takes place. Your baby is beginning to realise that objects still exist, even if they cannot be seen. Up to then, 'out of sight' literally means 'out of mind'. For example, at five months if your baby drops a toy from the cot, she will not look for it. It is as if the toy has disappeared from her awareness. By seven months, she is beginning to become aware that the toy may still be there and perhaps will look for it. By eight months, she will actively search for it.

These are very important changes. Now that your daughter knows that objects exist even when they are out of sight, and can be found by searching, she will be much more purposeful. She will begin to develop definite ideas about what she wants. She will start to demand the people and the things to which she has become attached and will not be easily deflected. For example, she will deliberately crawl across the room for a toy that she wants; she will search the cupboard for the biscuit tin; she may cry when you leave the room; she will shut her mouth tight if she does not like the food; she will demand her cuddly blanket before she goes to sleep. Your daughter is also learning to anticipate events. Now she knows that when you put on your coat, you are about to go out.

She may cling on to your legs and cry or try hard to influence your behaviour in some other way. Your daughter is beginning to have a will of her own, a process that will reach full flowering in the second year!

Language development

In the first year, your baby will be learning words rapidly, but this may not be obvious, because babies generally do not utter their first words until they are about a year old. However, they understand much more than they can say. As soon as they learn to anticipate events, they seem to understand the meaning of words like 'no!' 'hot!' and 'bye-bye'.

Yet long before she says her first words, your baby's language development is helped by your talking to her, particularly by talking to her about what interests her. In fact, the almost instinctive way parents talk to babies is exactly fitted to the development of language. All over the world parents talk to their babies in the same way: high-pitched, sing-song, short sentences, simple words, repeated sounds that mimic the baby's babbling (sounds beginning with m, p, b, t, d). Babies prefer listening to this baby-talk than to normal speech. Games such as 'Hide-and-Peepo' and 'Clap-hands' help children to learn about taking turns, a skill that is essential to conversation.

Parents instinctively help language development by treating their baby's smiles, yawns and sounds as part of a conversation. For example, a parent may say: 'Now, then, you're a hungry baby aren't you?' and pause, as if allowing the baby to answer, and then say: 'Of course you are', as if agreeing with the baby's imagined response. All this is not lost on the baby, who is learning and observing how conversations are carried on, but what is more important is that she is gratified that her 'responses' are treated like conversation. Occasionally you may feel silly or embarrassed when you hear yourself pretending to have a conversation with a very young baby, but don't worry. At every stage of their development, including this stage before they talk, children understand much more than they can express. Very soon you will hear all your conversation with your daughter repeated in her play with her dolls.

Emotional and social development

Many people of our parents' and grandparents' generation believed that babies did not have any real feelings; they cried when they were hungry or to exercise their lungs and smiled because they had wind. We now know that even young babies can express and respond to a very wide range of emotions, including fear, surprise, happiness, anger, disgust, interest and sadness. They are also sensitive to other people's feelings. Infants aged between one and three months will look away and fuss when they see a look of sadness or depression on their mother's face.

During the first six months of her life, your baby's emotions will become increasingly linked to the presence of other human beings. By about three months she is becoming more selective. Increasingly, you will evoke the biggest emotional reactions, negative and positive. You can make her happier, angrier, more frightened and more delighted than anybody else.

At three months, she still will be friendly to strangers, but at about six months, there is a noticeable change — the beginning of what is called 'stranger anxiety'. Your baby will become wary of strangers and may suddenly cry in fear when she is approached by an unfamiliar person. This fear will increase in strength up until about her first birthday. At around eight or nine months, the baby develops what is called 'separation anxiety', the fear of being left by her mother or father or even by her childminder. This will grow in strength until about fourteen months and may last until the second birthday.

These fears are universal. They appear at the same time in all cultures and are associated with a particular stage of the baby's intellectual development. As we saw earlier, this is the stage when babies get more knowledgeable about the world. They can now tell the difference between the familiar and the strange. They can remember and anticipate and they can see more reason to be afraid of things. The world is also opening up because of their new-found crawling skills. They discover things that frighten them, as well as things that delight them.

For all these reasons, babies become acutely aware of life's uncertainties. They are in critical need of a person who can be relied upon to respond predictably, to be there as a secure base. They cannot control this big, uncertain world by themselves. They need an adult whom they can influence and who in turn will control their world. This gives them a sense of control, a feeling that they can master the world. They are ready to form a passionate attachment to the person who will perform this role for them.

Crying

It has been estimated that one in ten babies cries a great deal, much more than their mothers consider normal. Mothers who work full-time in the home can spend up to twelve hours a day with a baby who is often crying. Learning to 'read' your baby's cry and knowing how to respond is a vital skill. Crying is your baby's only way of communicating her needs to you, especially in the early weeks before you have had a chance to get to know her temperament. It is vital for your confidence as a parent too. Once you know how to respond to your baby's cries, your self-esteem will blossom.

If you do not know why your baby is crying, you will become upset. Most parents who find themselves in that position feel guilty, angry, sorry for the baby, personally inadequate. This sometimes leads desperate parents to shake, and even to hit, the baby. Most parents know this is dangerous, and feel even worse about themselves, leading to a further loss of confidence.

Crying is a communication from your baby. What you have to do is decode the message. Here are some guidelines:

● Infants have three basic kinds of cries: hunger cries, anger cries and pain cries.

  The pain cry is the most distinctive because it is so sudden. Each individual cry is followed by a fairly long silence, while the baby is holding her breath. It is the most upsetting of all the cries.

  The hunger cry is also loud and insistent, but it has a more regular rhythm. Her cry will rise and fall, followed by her taking a breath and pausing, and then another cry. But the silent, breath-holding periods are shorter than in the pain cry. If very young babies wake hungry or are left waiting too long for a feed, their hunger cry will quickly become a pain cry.

  The anger cry may start as a whimper. It is not as loud or insistent as the hunger cry. It has a quavering quality and seems to end in mid-air, almost like a question mark. It appears to be asking: 'Is anybody out there going to pay me any attention?' If the whimper is not attended to, it may develop an angry quality and end up as a roar, as if saying 'Come here now!' or 'Stop what you are doing to me!'

● From about six months, babies begin to cry on purpose, to get something they want. This cry differs from earlier crying in that the baby will continue to cry until something specific happens, usually the return of the person whose departure has caused the crying.

- Each baby has a distinctive crying pattern. Depending on her temperament, she may go from whimper to roar instantly or quite slowly. She may cry in a scared way when she is overstimulated, or in a whimpery way when she is bored. She may cry regularly at particular times of the day.

- You will find it easier to interpret your baby's pattern of crying if you know her temperament. This will give you clues about which aspects of life she finds most stressful. For example, if she does not adjust well to change and tends to withdraw from new situations, she may find the transitional times of day a strain, when family members are leaving or returning from work. The solution is to find a way of anticipating her crying and to comfort her at these times. This may mean that you will have to hold her and play with her just before and for a while after the comings and goings. The dinner may be later, but you will not have a crying baby.

- The least helpful way of dealing with crying is to resist it. If this happens, the whimper will become a roar, the hunger cry will become a pain cry and the protest cry will become a wail of despair. In the meantime, you will have used up a lot of energy resisting the cry and the baby will be exhausted. Most times she will cry for far longer than your nerves will stand. By the time you get around to responding, you will have the mutual exhaustion and frustration to deal with, as well as the original cause of the crying.

- The tried and trusted ways of stopping a baby crying are:

  (a) rocking and movement and putting her to your shoulder. In fact, if you walk the room with her, you will get the rhythm exactly right.

  (b) warmth. Being warmly and securely wrapped, particularly in material that has a fuzzy surface, is soothing for babies. Swaddling a baby may also help by reducing the amount of involuntary, jerky movements of her arms and legs. This is particularly helpful for babies who react very quickly to any stimulation. Swaddling means wrapping the baby in a blanket securely so that her legs and arms are tucked in, like a parcel. Be careful not to wrap too tightly and to leave her hand free so that she can suck her fingers.

(c) rhythmic sound. The sound of a human heartbeat will soothe a crying baby — another good reason to hold her in your arms. Singing and talking in a gentle, repetitive way also helps. For times when you cannot attend immediately to your baby's crying, playing a tape recording of yourself singing a lullaby, or playing a music box, or a commercial tape of 'womb music' will comfort her temporarily.

(d) touch. Being held, fondled, stroked and patted will comfort a baby. You could also try gentle massage with baby or coconut oil, using gentle downward movements. This could be followed by a relaxing bath.

(e) playing. Your baby may be crying from boredom. Offer to be her playmate. With young babies, notice when she has tired of a toy and offer her another, rather than just piling toys in front of her. With older babies, ensure that her toys are in a place where she can choose which one she likes, but be careful to offer to play and wait for a response. Do not try to jolly her along if she does not feel like playing.

● Responding consistently and without unnecessary delay to your baby's crying makes sense. Babies who are responded to in this way for the first few months cry far less later on in their first year than babies who were ignored. At around twelve months they tend to cry very little and instead communicate with gestures, facial expressions and attempts to talk. In contrast, babies whose crying is not responded to frequently cry more often, and for longer periods, at twelve months of age and use fewer other means of communication. It is almost as if babies need to have their crying responded to before they learn other, more mature ways of communicating.

● It is also important to know when you can take no more. A danger sign is if you find yourself frequently interpreting your baby's crying as an angry rejection of you, almost

as if she were saying with her cry: 'You are not a good
mother/father'. If you are already feeling very stressed, this
feeling of being rejected by your baby can sometimes lead
to sudden and dangerous rage, followed by deep grief and
guilt. If you find yourself thinking like that, you need to
talk to somebody who can help you. This is not a sign that
you are a monster, as many parents fear. It is simply a sign
that you are in a classically stressful situation; you feel
unable to meet the demands that are being made on you,
but at the same time feel you cannot stop meeting those
demands.

The second year

The growth of independence

*I*n your child's second year, you and he share the same main goal. He passionately wants to become more independent, to have more control over his body and his activities, to do things for himself. That is what you want too. You were ready to respond to his every need when he was a helpless baby; now you want more co-operation. The main parenting task of the second year is to move smoothly to a more balanced partnership. Yet this transition is not easy, and towards the end of the second year many parents and their toddlers find themselves at cross-purposes for the first time.

This conflict increases over the second year from an average of three episodes per hour at fourteen months to six per hour at twenty-four months. Nearly all these conflicts are provoked by the child, and as toddlers grow older, they become even more self-assertive. By eighteen months they are much more likely than they were at the beginning of the second year to get angry, or even to laugh, when you try to talk sense to them. By twenty-four months, it's worse still.

The child's second year can often get bogged down in power struggles with the parent that not only get in the way of independence training, but can sour the relationship more permanently. The most common mistake is for parents to think of this toddler self-assertion as boldness, and to conclude that the solution is punishment.

The key to good parenting in the second year is to understand the way your child is developing, thinking and feeling. Everything the toddler is doing, even the things that are driving

43

you crazy, are part of his grand plan to grow into an independent, competent, loving and co-operative child. His method is trial-and-error. One minute he wants to be a big boy and do it himself; the next minute he wants to be a baby again. He wants to see how far he can take things (including your patience). Once more, his method is trial-and-error. That is the only way he can learn how the world works.

This learning is made doubly difficult by the fact that the toddler lives almost exclusively in the here-and-now. He is a creature of the moment and still has to develop the memory capacity to remember the lessons of yesterday and foresee the consequences of his actions. He cannot 'be reasonable' because he does not yet have the capacity to plan, wait and learn from experience.

It is only towards the end of the first year of his life that he begins to understand that you are a separate person. Up to then, he was not sure where he ended and you began. Now this feeling of separateness is good and bad news for the toddler. The good news is that he is independent and can actually begin to control his own body and actions. He is developing new skills every day and is bursting to try them out. The bad news is that he has lost that blissful security of infancy when you fulfilled all his needs. He is also discovering that, for all his new-found skills, he still has a lot to learn, and that the world can be a frustrating place.

However, no matter how frustrating, frightening and lonely it is to discover that he is a separate person, discover it he must. He has to stake out his territory and learn about 'me' and 'mine'. His method is simple: opposition. He finds out about himself by seeing how his actions affect others. He discovers that 'no' is an exciting word. 'No' is his first step away from you. Very young children have difficulty in saying 'yes'. Notice what happens when you ask him if he wants something. Very often he will not say 'yes' but will simply take what you offer or else wait for you to give it to him. He still does not know enough about himself to make a positive choice. 'Yes' is still being bound up with you, his provider. 'No' is finding out about himself.

The task for the toddler is to figure out the right amount of distance and closeness between you and him. If there is too much closeness, he will never grow up; too little and he will flounder. He teeters between the pleasure of being independent and the pain of losing you. Your task is much the same. You teeter between the pleasure of not having to do everything for him and the pain of knowing that he does not need you as much as when he was an infant. If you look at things in this way, you may see that the conflict between you is as much about sadness as about anger.

Your job as a parent in the second year is to continue to be his 'secure haven'. He can move away to learn and explore only as long as you are there to return to when he needs you. In effect you become your child's organiser. Your main task is to set up your lives together in such a way that the partnership you both want is likely to happen. The following points are worth bearing in mind:

- 'Organisation' is the key word. Your toddler will want to learn all the skills of being independent even if you give him no encouragement. The trick is to organise things in his daily life in such a way as to minimise needless frustrations. This can mean physically organising his toys and play space. It can mean structuring his day into manageable, enjoyable parts. It also means organising things so that you and he are not at odds.

- If you stay two steps ahead of your toddler, you can organise things in such a way that what you want becomes what he wants. Helping him to want what you want is not going to break his will. On the contrary, if you do it cleverly, it will seem to him that he is in control of his life, that he can do things, that he can handle frustration. Becoming competent, independent, co-operative and self-controlled will be the easy option for him. The way to do this is to teach him positively how to behave.

- Your short-term objective is to ease the so-called 'terrible twos'. The more important long-term goal is to help your child develop self-esteem. The foundation of his self-esteem is a feeling of confidence, a belief in himself, a feeling that he can control what happens to him. He will get these feelings day by day as he learns to master his small world. If he sees his delight and pleasure reflected in your eyes, these feelings will take strong root in his personality. Doing everything for him, because it is too time-consuming and irritating to wait for him to learn to do it himself, will buy temporary peace. So will insisting on him bending to your will — but you will pay a price later. Teaching, negotiating, co-operating, encouraging and staying positive will require a lot of hard work on your part. Doing things yourself and issuing orders is easier and requires less skill, but a great effort at this stage of your child's life will save hours of misery in the next phase of his development.

Discipline and punishment

One of the most common problems for parents is getting caught in a 'discipline trap'. This is the mistaken belief that the only way to get children to behave is by punishment, because they are motivated only by the fear of punishment. So the idea of discipline gets hopelessly mixed up with the idea of punishment.

Discipline means teaching children how to behave, and parents can learn positive skills to achieve that aim and to make it possible for their children to feel good about behaving well. This makes for happier family relationships and is also more effective than punishment. Punishment does not show the child what you want him to do. It simply stops him from doing something.

If you choose punishment as the way to discipline your child, you will have to be absolutely consistent. You will have to punish misbehaviour every time it occurs. Most parents are unable to keep this up. Children also get hardened by punishment and you will have to keep thinking of more effective penalties to make the required impact. This can create cycles of misbehaviour-punishment-defiance that will make for a very unpleasant, tense family life.

Punishment does have a limited role in child-rearing, especially as children get older. It really has very little role in the second year, because the toddler has not yet got the intellectual capacity to fully understand or anticipate punishment. It is better to concentrate on learning to be a positive parent.

Skills to encourage good behaviour

Your praise and attention are the magic ways to encourage your child to behave well, but there is a knack in using these skills:

- You must identify the behaviour that you want to encourage, whether it is playing quietly, helping to tidy up the toys or whatever.

- You must notice when your child is actually being quiet and praise him then. Many parents are afraid to do this, preferring to let sleeping dogs lie and hoping that the good behaviour will continue.

- Be consistent. Praise diligently and often.

- Tailor-make your praise, attention, rewards and punishment to suit your child's preferences.

- Pay more attention to the behaviour you want to encourage than to the behaviour you want to discourage.

Using praise and attention

Many parents are sceptical about the effectiveness of praising children, but if you master the technique, you will discover what a powerful effect it can have on your child's behaviour:

- Praise at the correct time — during or immediately after the behaviour you want to encourage.

- Be careful when you give attention, because negative attention can encourage undesirable behaviour. Scolding, glaring, sighing or passing 'smart' remarks are all ways of giving attention and they are doubly potent if this is the only way your child can get your attention. If he is a bright kid, he will continue to do whatever caught your attention.

- Say specifically what you are praising. This helps your child to know precisely what he needs to do to get your praise again. The skill is in learning to describe your child's behaviour. For example, if you want to encourage him to concentrate on a task, you might say: 'What a good boy you are now, looking at all the lovely pictures in your book, and sitting nice and quiet in your own little chair.' If you really want to encourage this behaviour, you could add the real prize of your time, by interrupting your activities for a few moments and letting the child point out the pictures in the book.

- Be positive and encouraging. Say to a child learning to button a coat or shirt: 'Good boy, keep trying . . . you're nearly there . . . now into the little hole . . . try again. Good.'

- Give praise for even the minor good things your child does, including those little jobs he is 'supposed to do'. One of the key differences between parents who have well-behaved children and those who say that their children never do anything right is that the former praise and encourage even fairly ordinary good conduct, thereby making possible the emergence of *really* good behaviour on exceptional occasions.

- Ensure that the praise is genuine. Many parents think that praise means ritually commending everything their child does, so their praise comes across as a routine matter. This is not lost on children. It is important to understand that praise is for behaviour that you genuinely want to encourage, and you should praise it sincerely. Initially, you may feel embarrassed, especially if you were not praised much by your own parents. Do not be tempted to cover up your embarrassment by sarcasm, as for example: 'What, you finally managed to go to the toilet. I can't believe it. . . .'

- Be physically affectionate when you give praise. Nobody grows out of the need for a reassuring hug, kiss or pat on the back.

- Find out what kind of praise your child prefers. Some children, particularly younger ones, love lavish praise together with hugs and kisses. Others prefer a serious acknowledgement of their virtue. For example, the parent stands still, looks serious and says solemnly: 'That is the best picture of a dog I ever saw. We must put it up on the fridge for everyone to see. . . .' Other children associate a particular pet name with praise and affection.

- Vary the kind of praise you use so that your commendation will always be effective.

Praising for not misbehaving

This is a variant of ordinary praise. The idea is to praise your child for not misbehaving. It reminds them that what they are doing is good, and of the bad behaviour they are avoiding. It is a good technique for preventing problems before they arise or before they get out of hand, and for teaching children in a positive way what they should not do. It is particularly useful for reducing fighting among brothers and sisters, and for curbing temper-tantrums. This technique is also helpful when your child seems to be misbehaving constantly and you find yourself nagging.

Praise your child's good behaviour by comparing it to previous troublesome behaviour. For example: 'Good boy. . . You asked for a biscuit instead of grabbing it. . . . Good boy, you are going to bed *without* complaining. . . . Well done for *not* asking for sweets in the supermarket.'

Praising for not misbehaving means identifying the situations where your child usually misbehaves and noticing when he is not doing it. Typically, your child is behaving well *just before* a bout of bad behaviour. For example, he may be playing well with a friend just *before* squabbling breaks out, or he will try to get your attention politely just *before* he freaks out with frustration because you will not listen. To stay ahead of your child, you have to notice these sequences of behaviour, and praise him for his good behaviour before the trouble breaks out. For example: 'Look how well you two are playing together without any silly fight that spoils the fun', or 'That's what I like to see, my little boy asking politely for something'.

Your praise must be descriptive. There is no point saying to your child: 'That's right. You are not doing it like you used to' because probably he will be none the wiser. It is better to say: 'That's right, you are putting a little on your spoon, instead of putting on too much which makes everything spill.'

Physical development in the second year

The most obvious development in your child's second year is his increasing mobility. From just being able to stand at thirteen months (the age when 90 per cent of babies can do it), he will be able to walk well at fourteen months, on average, walk backwards at twenty-one months, walk up steps at twenty-two months and kick a ball at twenty-four months. Yet your toddler is undergoing a very interesting psychological development at the same time. He is beginning to tolerate more distant forms of contact with you although he has an inbuilt radar. At one year he will move about seven metres from you; by age two this will have increased to about fifteen metres. He will also play more comfortably if he can see you, even though he may not look at you often. If you are temporarily out of his sight, he will increase his talking to you, as if substituting one form of contact for another. It is important for you to remember that you are still his 'safe haven', even though his new-found mobility may give the impression that he no longer needs your presence. He simply needs it in a different way.

Try to arrange your child's play space to suit his preferred safe distance. The ideal arrangement is provided by the average suburban kitchen-cum-diningroom. If you can block off exits, and remove fragile and dangerous objects, the diningroom can become his space. It is sensible to have his important toys and books there, near at hand. You may be dismayed to hear that the longest period of sustained play with a single toy at age two is about thirty seconds! Better to have a diningroom that looks like a toy warehouse than a bored and frustrated toddler.

Feeding problems

At about one year your child may lose the voracious appetite he had as an infant. Now that he will not eat everything that is put in front of him, you may worry that he is not eating enough. You can avoid feeding problems by keeping sensible guidelines in mind.

The golden rule is not to turn feeding and mealtimes into battlegrounds of coaxing, scolding and temper-tantrums (your own as well as your toddler's). Children love a good argument about eating because they sense they have you where they want you. Parental anxiety is a sure guarantee that they will get your attention. The combination of a toddler's will and a parent's worry that their child is not eating enough provides a fertile breeding ground for the development of feeding problems.

- Save yourself the worry about whether he is getting enough food by realising that if he is offered a wide range of foods, your toddler will choose a balanced diet. It may not be balanced at any one meal, but it will be balanced in an overall way. Remember, in order to thrive in the first two years, all your child needs is about fifty calories per day per pound of body weight. For example, a slice of cheese and two slices of bread, a pint of milk, an orange and an egg will provide most of the vitamins, minerals, protein and calories the average toddler needs each day. The important thing is to include in his food protein, carbohydrates, calcium, minerals and vitamins. If you are uncertain about what foods are in each category, and what constitutes a good balanced diet, consult your family doctor, health visitor or reliable family health book. If, for example, your toddler hates meat, give him other forms of protein like cheese or fish or milk. If he hates vegetables, give him fruit.

- Allow your child as much control as possible over the way he eats. At this stage, fingers, fork, spoon, in any creative combination he chooses are fine. All you need do is offer the opportunity and encouragement to learn to use cutlery in the conventional way so that he can try them if he prefers. Allow him to experiment and combine his food in any way he chooses, even in ways you find off-putting. It is he who should enjoy it, not you.

- Encourage him to try out new foods, for example, by cutting food into neat finger pieces, chunks, cubes and arranging the bits attractively; or grating food into soft, squishy 'mountains'. This does not mean going to a lot of trouble with recipes — unless you love cooking — and then feeling resentful if he will not eat.

- Ask him only to taste new food, not necessarily to swallow or finish it.

- Praise and encourage your child when he is eating enjoyably and well, and when he tries to use cutlery, even if he does not hold it correctly.

- Do not teach him to be an over-eater by insisting on a clean plate or encouraging him to finish off the morsels. It is important that he should learn to attend to the signals in his own body that tell him when he is full.

Keep mealtimes pleasant. They are an opportunity to talk with your child. Do not expect him to sit through the whole family meal, but include him as often as you can.

Sleeping

Toddlers are bursting with energy, but they are much better at starting an activity than at stopping it. They are better at speeding up than slowing down. This applies to most of the skills they develop during this second year. Observe, for example, how difficult they find it to walk slowly on a straight line, or to draw a straight line slowly. 'Go' signals are easier for them than 'Stop' signals, whether the signal is coming from you or from inside their own bodies. One consequence is that very often they get over-tired. Your task is to set up a predictable routine, until such a time as he gets better at regulating his own bodily rhythms. Managing sleeping, waking, naps and bedtimes is a critical part of the second year. You can minimise bedtime problems by keeping sensible guidelines in mind.

- Sticking to the same bedtime every night is sensible. With an older, school-going child, you may want to vary bedtime at weekends, but this often leads to endless arguing and negotiation.

- Choose bedtime carefully. You will need to take account of the total number of hours your particular child needs (not the typical toddler or the child next door), including the number and length of naps and other family or personal demands. For example, if you work outside the home, you may wish to spend a few hours with your toddler when you come home. This is fine if he is happy and alert up until that bedtime, but you cannot then expect him to take happily to being put to bed earlier on the nights you want to go out. Having worked out the bedtime that suits your child, yourself and the other members of the family, stick to it.

- If you have not done so already, establish a bedtime routine. This should start about half-an-hour before. You signal to the child, in the same way every night, that bedtime is coming up, for example, by saying: 'Time for bed soon, but first upstairs for your bath.' Other parts of the routine might be getting into pyjamas, saying goodnight to a few toys, tucking in Teddy, reading a story, turning off the light, singing a lullaby, and then kissing the child goodnight and leaving the room. Try not to vary the routine once it has been established.

- If your child fusses or starts to cry at the end of the routine, wait outside his room for a while to give him a chance to settle. Only if the crying intensifies should you go back in. Repeat the last parts of the routine (assuming there is nothing specific that is making him cry) and leave again. Repeat the process until he settles, no matter how long it goes on. This is very hard advice to follow, but it is worth persisting. Be prepared to do it for up to two weeks, although it is likely to solve the problem in a shorter time.

- Do not bring your child downstairs again. This may give short-term relief to your jangled nerves, but you can say goodbye to any private time if you do. If you try to reintroduce the old routine he will pull out all the stops to get you to bring him down again.

Toilet-training

One of the major issues in the second year is deciding when to start toilet-training. Many parents cannot wait to start. This is understandable; most find changing nappies a chore. Yet, in their anxiety to get the child trained, many parents store up needless stress for him and for themselves. The single biggest mistake is to start too soon. Almost inevitably this will end in tears and frustration, and if it is handled badly, it can create emotional problems for the child later. Bear in mind the following guidelines before you embark on toilet-training:

- By age three most children are fully toilet-trained, though occasional accidents may occur up to age five and beyond.

- Many parents, particularly first-time parents, have unrealistic expectations about when toilet-training can be started and completed. Some plan to begin before the child is sixteen months of age and expect to have the job done before the child is two years old.

- Coercive toilet-training, where the child is compelled to go to the toilet, can result in enuresis (persistent wetting in older children) or encopresis (persistent soiling in older children).

- The decisive thing in toilet-training is the child's readiness. He is ready to be toilet trained when (a) he has reached a certain physical level of maturity. A clue to his possible readiness is if he has good enough co-ordination to walk well without assistance and to pick up small objects easily; (b) he has sufficient bladder control. A clue is if he empties his bladder completely at one time, generally has a dry nappy for several hours and, most important, indicates in some way, by making a face, or clutching himself, that he is about to empty his bladder or his bowels; (c) if he has sufficient understanding of language. A clue is if he is able to understand and carry out two instructions given simultaneously ('Put Teddy on the chair and bring Dolly over to me'); (d) if he is showing a readiness to do other things for himself, like helping to dress himself; (e) if he is secure and getting on well with you.

  For most children, the first four elements of 'readiness' seem to peak after twenty months, but it is more sensible to wait until these new developments have become firmly established at around twenty-four months. The last element (e) is an individual matter. If your child is under particular stress at this time, perhaps because of the arrival of a new baby, or some family problem, it is better to delay toilet-training until your relationship with your child is on a more secure footing.

- Toilet-training proper, then, belongs to the third rather than to the second year. Children over twenty-four months are more easily and quickly trained than children under twenty-four months. If you start later, you will achieve the same result, faster and with less wear-and-tear all round.

- During the second year you can begin to prepare the child for toilet-training by teaching him self-help skills in dressing, helping him to understand and follow simple instructions and introducing him to the idea of toilets. You can let him accompany you to the toilet occasionally. You can talk about going to the toilet and introduce the words for urine and faeces that you find acceptable.

- At around eighteen months, you can introduce him to the potty. Tell him what it is for. Put it in a corner of the room where he spends most of his day. Once he gets the idea, you could suggest he sits teddy on it and invent a game in which toys go to the toilet, changing nappies and so on.

- When he indicates that he is about to empty his bowel or bladder by making a face or turning red, you could suggest that he does it in the potty. Do not insist. Remember that your long-term goal is to have him in control of his bodily functions, so it is vital not to interfere with his sense of control.

- Start with bowel-training, since this is easier for the child. Observe over a period of days when he is likely to have a bowel movement. You could try removing his nappy and suggesting that he sit on the potty. Do not keep him there for much longer than five minutes. If he performs as requested, praise him. If he does not, be matter-of-fact. Try again the next day. If the child is introduced in this relaxed way, he is likely to train himself in a matter of weeks with no fuss. If he has difficulty making the connection between what he does in his nappy and what he is supposed to do in the potty, you could try emptying the soiled nappy into the potty, again in a relaxed way, explaining all the time what you are doing.

- The first step in bladder-training is to allow the child to go without nappies for a while each day. Make this pleasant for the child by pointing out how freely he can move and the nice feeling of sitting bare-bottomed on the floor. Encourage him to use the potty. If he does this successfully for a few days, dispense with nappies during the day while he is at home and use trainer pants instead. Do not make a fuss about cleaning up after accidents; the idea is to keep the whole process relaxed. Once things have been going smoothly for a few weeks, with few daytime accidents, dispense with the trainer pants and with the nappies, except at night.

How your toddler thinks

Your toddler's intelligence develops in leaps and bounds during his second year. From twelve to eighteen months, he will go through what is called the 'little scientist' stage. He is determined to discover the possibilities of his world by experimenting. This is how he understands how things work. Having discovered what he can do with an object, he immediately sets about seeing what else he can do with it. Toddler thinking is along the lines of: 'What will happen if I turn my plate upside down? . . . put my finger in the dog's eye? . . . look at the TV upside down?' No matter how exasperated you are when he 'experiments' with your best perfume, it is vital to understand that this is not misbehaviour. His method is trial-and-error, and toddlers have to experiment if they are to develop intellectually.

Your job as a parent is to organise his 'laboratory' for him. That means providing appropriate play materials, a variety of stimulation and, most important, your own participation as a playmate. If you do this, you are laying the best possible foundation for his later intellectual achievement. Providing appropriate play materials does not mean buying expensive toys. Toddlers can experiment with all kinds of ordinary household things, such as boxes, saucepans, plastic bottles and home-made play-dough. Most important is your involvement in play. Toddlers need the typical rough-and-tumble play of fathers and the quieter, conversational play of mothers. In particular, reading to your child every day is the best guarantee that he will turn out to be an articulate and competent schoolchild. Books are probably among the best things you can give your toddler.

Between eighteen and twenty-four months, your toddler has developed a new intellectual skill. He is beginning to solve simple problems in his mind, without having to resort to actual experiments. You will see him stop an activity in order to work out how to solve a problem. For example, he wants to open the door into the hall, but cannot because he has a toy in his hand. So, he puts the toy on the ground, opens the door with both hands, picks up the toy, closes the door and goes out. Mission accomplished. However, a problem arises on the way back. Before he opens the door, he puts the toy on the ground, but now sees in his mind's eye that if he opens the door it will catch on the toy. He solves the problem by putting the toy further back. A few short months previously he might have tried to pull the door over the toy and so become frustrated. Such an example makes it easier to understand how frustrating the smallest task can be for a toddler and why tantrums are inevitable.

The child has a growing ability to create mental images of things and actions that are not actually in view. The most obvious sign that he has reached this stage is his ability to pretend; the cardboard box can be a car, a house, a mountain. As well as that he can begin mentally to combine an action from one situation (being driven in a car) with an action in another (sitting on a box), but this time he can pretend to be the driver.

These developments mean that your child is beginning to remember, to imagine. Out-of-sight does not automatically mean out-of-mind; he will look more systematically for something that has disappeared. If he is interrupted in the middle of something, he can go back to it afterwards and continue where he left off. It is the first step towards a more thoughtful, less impulsive way of responding to the world, the first step away from the totally here-and-now world that the toddler inhabits. Still, it is only a first step, and it is as well to bear in mind that these changes begin to happen only at around eighteen months.

Language development

Your child's language ability is also developing. By eighteen months the average toddler will have a vocabulary of up to 50 words; by twenty-four months this will have risen to more than 200 words, and he can now combine words into two-

word sentences. This rapid development in part is connected
to his new thinking skills. He can form an image of something,
even when it is not there. This makes it possible for him, for
example, to connect the word 'car' with an actual car, whether
the car is there or not. His memory of objects is so new and
important to him that a lot of his language at this stage is about
things being 'all gone'. You can help your child enlarge his
inner world by reading and telling stories. For the first time
your child can imagine. Capitalise on it. Reading stories to him
will help his language development, provide a much-needed
quiet time and establish a reading habit that will stand him and
you in great stead when he reaches that later stage in middle
childhood when boredom may become a problem.

Here are some other ways you can help your child's language
development:

- Treat you child's communications as meaningful, even if
you do not fully understand the words he uses or if they
are mispronounced. If the child says 'Dwo', pointing at
his shoe (a favourite first word), say something like: 'Yes,
your shoe. That's a nice, blue shoe.' Then wait for a
response. Continue to chat about the shoe if he is still
interested. If not, talk about what is now interesting him.

- Talk as you do things with your child. For example: 'Now,
we're putting on your nice red jumper.' Elaborate your
descriptions if he seems interested: 'Your jumper is red but
my jumper is white. What about Daddy's jumper? That's
blue.'

- Use ordinary speech yourself, but do not correct his
grammatical mistakes. Simply reinterpret what he says and
repeat it in conversation, using the right grammar. For
example, if your toddler points to a picture and says
'mouses', you say. 'Yes. There are two grey mice and they
have big, long whiskers.'

- Do not assume that because he has only a few words he
cannot understand a great deal of speech or is not listening
to what you say. Just wait until he comes out with a few
choice profanities and you will have evidence of his
listening and learning ability. Meanwhile, keep talking to
him, as long as he seems interested.

● Reading nursery rhymes will delight him and introduce him to the sounds and music of the language in the best possible way.

How your toddler develops emotionally

The toddler's sense of self, his self-awareness, develops gradually over the first two years. Even at eight months, babies do not seem to know where their bodies end and where somebody else's begins, as you can see when your baby grabs a toy in another child's hand and reacts with surprise when the toy 'won't come'. By twelve months, your baby will be well aware that the other child is a distinct person, and may even take a swipe at him if toy 'won't come'. But he will be well into his second year before he learns that 'the baby' he sees in the mirror is himself.

This emerging sense of self ushers in a new range of emotions, such as shame, guilt, jealousy and pride. Now that your toddler is getting the idea that he and other people are separate, it makes possible the first stirrings of true affection and defiance. His most important struggle is for autonomy — the right to rule his own body and actions. If he succeeds, he feels pride and confidence. If he fails, he feels shame and doubt. Your role is to organise things so that he can learn to stand on his own feet, but at the same time you must protect him from needless experiences of shame and self-doubt.

Understanding toddler psychology can guide parents in the way they handle their child. Here are some practical suggestions:

● Child-proof the environment: toddlers are impulsive. To enable your toddler to experiment and play in safety, you should (a) remove dangerous and fragile household objects; (b) set clear 'off limits' in the house and (c) teach children about danger from the beginning, even if you have to keep repeating warnings.

● Create and keep to a predictable schedule and to established routines of eating, sleeping and playing. What you are doing is creating an external structure that will make up for his still unreliable memory structure. Toddlers want many aspects of their environment to stay put, so that they can concentrate more easily on learning about the world. That is why you have to be careful how much novelty to introduce. Too much will interfere with his ability to cope, too little will slow his learning. One rule of thumb is to introduce one novelty at a time, waiting and observing his reaction. Do not, for example, start toilet-training or put him in a crèche at the same time as a new baby arrives. Start before, or leave it until he is ready. Another rule of thumb is to take account of a recent increase in temper-tantrums or special fears, especially nightmares. Try to see if there have been any recent changes in his routine, though the changes may seem minor.

- Help your toddler to learn problem-solving skills. Toddlers have difficulty organising their activities; they are capable of concentrating only in short bursts. Playing with an adult partner will help him to develop the skills he needs. You can suggest ways in which he can solve problems, and if he is in real difficulty, show him. You can show him how to organise and combine his toys into a game. By letting him share your adult activities, you can teach him the different steps in a routine like making a bed, cleaning a car, sorting the groceries. What you are really teaching him is how to think and plan in an organised way.

- Help your toddler to learn to make choices. Since it is hard for him to anticipate consequences, you will have to make most of the important choices for him, but you can allow him to make choices when they are possible. For example, you can lay out a few T-shirts on the bed and he can choose which one to wear. You can allow him to pick his favourite flavour of yoghurt.

- Help your toddler learn to control his emotions. The first skill to teach is the ability to accept frustration. This requires learning to wait and controlling the build-up of feelings. Toddlers have great difficulty doing either.

The best strategy is to minimise any unnecessary delays in the toddler's day. It is worth going to almost any trouble to do this. Before you plan any activity or outing, reflect on what kind of delays are likely, ask yourself how you are going to cope with your toddler's inevitable frustration, and then ask yourself whether the activity is worth it or if there is another way of doing it.

Coping with frustration

You can help your toddler to accept that frustration is a factor of life:

- Make him see that sometimes waiting is worthwhile: the car journey will result in a day at the beach; the walk to the shops will result in an ice-cream; waiting until you are finished preparing the dinner will result in a special game with you. When you promise him something if he waits patiently, always keep your promise. A child who experiences too many broken promises will come to believe that it is not worth waiting for anything, that it is not worth postponing an immediate pleasure for a delayed reward. As a consequence, he will not stick at a hard task for the future reward of mastering some skill. This can create all kinds of difficulty in school later.

- Build up his capacity to wait. Teach him to distract himself by doing something else while waiting, and as he gets older, to distract himself by thinking about something else. Older children who can tolerate delays and frustrations often have learned to control what they think about while they wait. They have learned to distract themselves by singing, reading, talking to themselves, inventing little games, learning to relax or nodding off for a while. Your toddler is too young to do these things, but it is not too early to teach him. If you distract him initially, he will imitate you later.

- Set an example yourself. Obviously you are a poor example if you have emotional outbursts yourself; but even if you are a model of self-control, it will not be obvious to your toddler how you do it. Make it easier for him to learn by saying out loud when you have to, or choose to, delay doing something: 'I can wait for that' or 'I could have this snack, but if I look carefully on all the shelves of the fridge, I will find something far nicer'.

- Watch for the build-up of tension and excitement and intervene before it becomes an emotional outburst. It pays to observe your toddler and to get to know his particular 'boiling-over' point. Many parents do not see the connection between the build-up of tension and excitement and a subsequent tantrum.

- Set clear limits for your toddler in the pace of his activities and in the expression of his frustration. He will find it comforting to know that somebody can be counted on to stop him before he goes too far. A minority of parents have the very wrong-headed idea that if they let their toddler really lose control and damage something or hurt himself, this will teach him a lesson. It will not. Toddlers do not have the intellectual capacity to make this connection. All that will happen is that the toddler will suffer a crisis of confidence that will slow down his learning.

- Teach the necessary skills to your toddler so that he has the best chance of succeeding at any task. That is the best way for him to avoid frustration. The key is to think small. For example, with regard to learning to dress himself, start by teaching him to pull up his trousers. You first put both his legs in and pull the trousers up to his knees. Then all he has to do is pull them up the rest of the way. The next step is to teach him to put one leg into his trousers, but only teach him to do that when the first step has been mastered. Then, think out all the tiny steps he has to learn next, up to the final one of putting on his shoes.

- Teach him other ways to release his pent-up feelings. Many children find that singing at the top of their voices, pounding play-dough, or running 'races' around the garden will defuse a build-up of frustration.

Coping with tantrums

I have left this until last, because if you are to cope sensibly with tantrums you must have some understanding of your toddler's make-up. That, in turn, will help you to accept that some tantrums are inevitable.

- Cultivating a philosophical attitude towards tantrums is the first coping skill to learn. Do not waste your time apologising to disapproving shoppers in the supermarket if your child has a tantrum there. Simply assume that they have no experience with children or that they are suffering from memory difficulties about their own children at that stage.

- Try to prevent as many outbursts as possible by following the guidelines above.

- When your child does have a tantrum, concentrate on containing it. The best way is to hold the child gently but firmly in your arms. If that is not possible, concentrate on removing anything that might get in his way, get damaged or hurt him. If you are in a crowded place, try to remove him to a quiet corner or outside.

- Try not to get angry. Anger feeds anger. This is very, very hard advice to follow. If you feel yourself getting angry, you may have to put a physical distance between yourself and the child, assuming that the tantrum is happening somewhere safe. For example, if you are at home, you could put your child in his normal play space, and go out into the hall or bathroom yourself. Count up to fifty. Check that he is safe. If you are still angry, repeat the procedure. Do not go near him until you feel in control again. If you are in a public place, breathe deeply, count to ten, ignore passersby and concentrate on saying soothing things to your child like 'OK, darling. OK. It's going to be alright. Mummy/Daddy is here'. Call him by his pet name if he has one. This may be the last thing you feel like saying, but it will have the effect of calming you too.

- Do not let his tantrum change your mind. If he threw a tantrum because you would not give him something or allow him to do something, do not change your mind no matter how upset you both are. Even if you think, with hindsight, that it was unreasonable to refuse him, stick to your guns. Otherwise, he will learn an important lesson: tantrums work.

- Do not let the possibility of a tantrum make you treat him differently in situations where you worry about the embarrassment, for example in supermarkets, when you have special visitors or when you are with a disapproving friend or relative. He will sense that you are treating him with 'kid gloves' and this will interest him greatly. He will sense what is up and may decide to test how far he can push you.

The pre-school years

A t some stage during your child's third year you will find yourself saying to somebody: 'You know, she really is *much better* than she used to be.' By her fourth year, you will find yourself doing things that you have not done since before she was born. You have reached the (relatively) tranquil slopes of the pre-school years. During those years, day by day, your child is beginning to be 'more herself', more loving, relaxed, independent and competent. She wants to accomplish things, not just to assert her independence, as she did when she was a toddler. Her enthusiasm to grow up will know no bounds. She wants to learn about the world, to understand about being a girl and a boy, being a parent, being a friend. She wants to learn about the work adults do and imitate their actions in play. She wants to learn to be good, to understand the difference between right and wrong.

The way she will accomplish most of these things is through play. Growing up is a game. Running, chasing and doing physical 'tricks' will develop her body. Word games and playing out ideas will develop her mind. Through pretend play she will develop her understanding of how the world works. Her new stage of intellectual development, especially her language development, will make it all possible. The single biggest change is that she is now able to talk about almost anything that happens to her.

Physical development in the pre-school years

The most obvious development is in her size and shape. She is longer and slimmer. Her body now has much the same proportions as an adult. However, the most important physical development is not obvious — the maturation of her brain. During childhood, her brain develops faster than any other part of her body. By age five, her brain will have reached 90 per cent of its adult weight, despite the fact that her body is approximately only one-third of its adult weight. The parts of her brain that control eye-hand co-ordination, focused attention and concentration develop rapidly in the pre-school years.

During these years your child will have a higher activity level than at any other time in her life. Her skill in using her body, in climbing, running, jumping and throwing improves dramatically. She will practise these skills wherever she is. She will teach herself, or learn with other children. All you have to do is provide her with a safe play-space, suitable equipment and playmates.

Your daughter will still have difficulty controlling her fine body movements. Pouring milk from a jug into a glass without spilling it, tying a bow, using a knife and fork require muscular control and judgement that she still does not have, because her brain has not reached that stage of maturation. You need to bear these physical limitations in mind when you choose toys, clothes and eating utensils for your daughter. Velcro fastenings and big buttons, for example, will make it easier for her to dress herself. Delicate toys or jigsaw puzzles with easily crushed pieces are best avoided. What best helps the pre-school child to become finely co-ordinated is drawing and making marks on paper. You can encourage her to use crayons and markers so that she will practise these skills. There is no better preparation for formal learning in school in the years ahead.

You will notice that, in many ways, your daughter plays differently than boys of her own age. Boys and girls develop a strong preference for playmates of their own sex, and this preference will last right through the school years. The girls will play more at arts and crafts, at games that require co-operation and taking turns, and in small groups of two or three. The boys will play more outside, often in larger groups, in physical, energetic games, like chasing, rough-and-tumble play and in attempts to establish dominance one over the other. Not only do children play differently with children of the same sex than they do with children of the opposite sex, but they interact less when they are in mixed-sex pairs. Even when adults encourage them to play together, children will revert to their own-sex playmates when left on their own.

Intellectual development in the pre-school years

Your child has reached a new stage of thinking — she has become capable of symbolic thought. Her mind is no longer limited by what she can do or see or feel; instead, she thinks in symbols — words. Knowing what words mean, she can move about mentally, in the past and the future, as well as in the present. The word 'horse' conjures up an image in her mind. She can now remember what a horse is, she can talk about it. The image will call up other images in her mind to do with horses and animals, and all sorts of ideas and information about them. Her mind is set free by words. By age two she will have more than 200 words. She is learning between six and ten words a day. By age five, she can learn almost any new word or phrase if it is explained to her with examples and she hears it used in the right context. This is a critical age for language development. Talking to your daughter, including her in adult conversations and giving her as many books as you can afford will give her the essential raw ingredients for learning.

This new intellectual development is best expressed in the quality of your child's 'pretend' play. Not only can she transfer any object into whatever she chooses, she can play solely in imagination.

Nevertheless, she still has some way to go before she will think logically. For example, she may know that three sweets and two sweets make five, but will not see that the reverse is also true, that is, if you take away two sweets from five sweets you will be left with three. She will tend to think about one idea at a time, to the exclusion of other ideas. For example, she may think that the tallest child must also be the oldest and the best. She will have difficulty understanding cause and effect, because she focuses on one part of an event rather than on the relationship between them. Thus, she will say with utter sincerity that a glass broke because it wanted to (not because she knocked it over), or that she hurt her knee because the chair hit her. Because of her focus on one aspect of things, she thinks in either/or terms; you must be either good or bad, a mother or a daughter, and so on.

Emotional and social development

There is also rapid development in your daughter's self-awareness, self-confidence and self-understanding. She becomes more socially skilled. Like all pre-schoolers, she will have a very positive view of herself and will overestimate her own ability to do almost anything. She is the best singer in the world, she could climb a mountain, she could win any race. Even when she fails at some everyday thing, she will confidently predict that she will do better next time, unless, of course, it is specifically pointed out to her how poorly she has done. Then, she will be less confident.

It is as if her incredible energy gives her the confidence to try anything, forget failure quickly and start new activities with exuberance. Yet, her wondrous initiative is balanced by a new capacity for guilt. If her efforts result in failure or criticism, she feels guilty. So, for all her self-confidence, your pre-schooler must be protected from unnecessary failure and despondency, just as diligently as she was protected from falling down and hurting herself while she was a toddler.

Gradually, as she becomes more herself, she will move away from her exclusive attachment to her parents. But, at the same time, she is building her sense of a separate self by identifying with you: modelling her actions and reactions on yours, internalising your voice and making it hers. You will actually hear her say to herself what once you said to her: 'Oh! I must be careful of the step. I might fall' or 'I am a good girl and eating all my dinner'. She will be more capable of understanding your point of view, and of responding with sympathy and concern to your feelings. She will passionately want to help you do everything, because her new-found confidence makes her feel capable of almost anything, and helping you makes her feel grown-up.

Above all, as she is becoming more and more aware of herself and other people, your child will become more sensitive to praise and blame. The way you handle this as a parent will have a very important effect on her self-esteem. Your task is to devise a style of parenting that will help her to stay confident, and to become independent, happy with herself and happy with others.

Three styles of parenting

As a parent, you have always to keep two goals in mind: how best to deal with your child's immediate demands, and how best to prepare your child for the next stages of growing up. What you do at one stage will affect what happens later. For example, if you respond readily to your baby in the first year, you are more likely to have a pre-school child who is compliant with your wishes. If you are relatively indifferent to your pre-school child's needs, it is more likely that, as a teenager, your child will have poor self-control and difficulties with relationships. Any investment now will pay dividends later, particularly in the adolescent years. It is as if children, while they are growing up, have a quota of time and attention that they need from their parents. If they do not get this in the early years, their problems in later years will ensure that they will get your attention then, whether you like it or not. There is no fool-proof recipe for parenting, but some styles of parenting have happier outcomes than others.

Researchers have identified three styles of child-rearing, 'authoritarian', 'authoritative' and 'permissive', and have shown that these produce very different types of child behaviour.

Authoritarian child-rearing: Parents emphasise obedience, respect for authority, work, tradition and law-and-order. They try to shape and control their children in accordance with these absolute standards. Their children are judged by how well they are living up to these standards, rather than by their personal accomplishments. Such parents do not approve of verbal give-and-take.

Authoritative child-rearing: Parents try to direct children in a rational way, explaining the reasons for their demands and discipline but using power when necessary. They do not concentrate so much on principle ('You always have to obey your parents') as on the issue at hand ('You have to behave in this particular way now and this is why'). They expect their child to conform to adult demands, but will tolerate verbal give-and-take and expect their child to be independent.

Permissive child-rearing: Permissive parents try to behave in an accepting, positive way towards their child's impulses and actions. They use little punishment, make few demands for household responsibility, allow children to regulate their own activities. They try not to control their children. They use reasoning, but not overt power to achieve their objectives.

Children of *authoritarian* parents tend to be obedient, orderly and not to be aggressive, if their parents were also warm and accepting, but they seem to be paying a price. They tend to be withdrawn, a bit joyless, and lacking in understanding and sympathy for other people. They are timid and not persistent in pursuing their goals. If their parents punished them a lot the children tend to be low in self-esteem, lacking in independence, originality, and self-control, and will do things only for reward or punishment rather than because it is the right or wrong thing. The result of this kind of child-rearing seems to be worse for boys than for girls. Boys reared in this way tend to be defiant, angry and likely to lose interest in achievement during their early school years.

Children of *authoritative* parents tend to be happy, self-reliant and able to meet challenges well. They are independent yet socially responsible and enjoy good relationships with friends. They tend to set standards for themselves and try to meet them. When they meet difficulties they persist in their efforts and show initiative and originality.

Children of *permissive* parents tend to be immature. They are low in self-reliance and self-control. They are not particularly independent or socially responsible. Boys may also be angry and defiant.

Teaching your child how to behave is the key to good discipline. Your child will co-operate with you in learning how to behave because she is so eager to model herself on you. How much she wants to do this depends on how much she respects and admires you. By being responsive to her needs and freely giving of your love, you effectively *earn* your child's respect and willingness to behave as you wish her to. There is nothing wrong with trying to earn her respect. After all, you cannot make her respect you. You can only make her fear you.

Your short-term goal is to get your daughter to behave well, but your long-term objective is to ensure that she will develop high standards and strong inner controls for herself. In other words, you hope that gradually your voice (urging her to do her best, to resist temptation and scolding her if she does wrong) will become her inner voice — the still, small voice of conscience.

This is how it happens. Your child gradually begins to monitor her own behaviour, to make it fit in with her view of herself. She moves from believing 'I'm being good because my parents say I have to be' to believing 'I'm being good because *I am* a good girl'. She moves from saying 'I'm not doing a bad thing because I'm afraid I will be punished' to saying 'I'm not doing a bad thing because it would make *me* feel bad. . . .' You can see, if you look at it like that, that her self-esteem is critical. To be effective, your discipline has to help her develop self-esteem. The more highly she thinks of herself, the higher the standards she will set for herself. Doing wrong would demean her in her own eyes.

As a parent, you are your child's mirror. If she looks into your eyes and sees that you regard her with affection, respect and trust, she will come to think of herself as worthy of affection, respect and trust. Your child is developing a looking-glass self.

Standards and rules in the pre-school years

Clear and consistently enforced standards and rules help your child to know what is required of her. She will feel confident, not anxious, about how you are likely to react. These rules occasionally may irritate her, but in time she will see that they are a sign of your concern for her welfare. At the next stage of her development, if things have gone well, she will mostly agree with your views about how you want her to behave. Finally, you will stop being the 'bad guy' and become the benevolent, wise parent of the school-going years. There is a lot at stake in how sensibly you set your standards and make your rules during the pre-school years.

- Set standards and make rules that are within your child's capabilities. This sounds obvious, but some parents are unsure about what children are capable of at particular ages and have unrealistically high standards. Many children do not comply with their parents' requests because they are based on unreasonable rules. For example, the rule 'you should always keep yourself clean' or 'you should always be quiet' cannot be followed if your child is to get on with the business of childhood, which is playing.

A rule such as 'you must always share your toys' is unreasonable because, like yourself, your child has a right to her own things and should be able to choose whether or not to share. Of course you can encourage her to share, but you must understand the stage she is at. The pre-school child likes to stake her territory. This is part of her definition of self and she will claim almost everything as her own: 'my toys', 'my house', 'my teacher'.

You can help your child to share by making her understand how other people feel. You can point out how it feels when she wants something and somebody else will not share. You can point out how much fun it can be when you share toys. You can help her decide which toys are never to be shared, like a favourite doll, and suggest that she leaves it in a special place, out of sight, when she has friends over. She may be happy then to share the rest of her toys.

● The fewer general rules you have the better. It is hard for young children to understand when to apply a general rule. If you tell a child 'you always have to obey adults' she may feel compelled, for example, to comply with an adult's sexual demands, as well as his instruction to keep it a secret.

Sometimes rules are helpful: about bedtime, watching TV, fighting, mealtimes, hygiene, and behaviour in public places. Laying down a few general rules about moral behaviour is also helpful, for example, rules about telling the truth and having respect for other people and for other people's property. Often rules simply encourage good habits; like all habits, they are more easily acquired if the child has a regular, organised daily schedule. If you are trying to teach complex moral reasoning and behaviour, your only hope of doing it successfully is if you are actively interested and involved in your child's life and in her problems.

● Training to meet the standards you set is crucial. Training in independence and self-help skills, dressing for instance, may be obvious, but children also need training in how to settle disputes without fighting, in learning to tolerate frustration and in helping others. An important skill to teach children is how to notice that some action is needed and showing them what they can do to solve the problem without creating a fresh problem. You may need to point out to your child how to notice that trouble is brewing between her and her friends (raised noise, squabbling, angry outbursts, one child withdrawing), suggest the source of the problem (the game has gone on too long, the game excludes one child, there is only one doll's pram and three children) and help her to suggest a solution (thinking of a new game, doing something quieter for a while, getting the other children to go home and fetch more toys).

● Vigilance is all important. There is not much point in making rules and then not ensuring that they are being followed. Obviously you cannot be vigilant all the time and children are amazingly skilful at escaping notice. But, unfortunately, only the reasonably vigilant parent can succeed in enforcing rules consistently. This is a good reason for having *only* as many rules as you are capable of enforcing.

● Involve your child in family decisions as much as possible. There are many aspects of family life where, with some forethought and skill, you can find ways of giving her choices. If the rule is that she watches only one hour's television a day, you can allow her choose from a few suitable programmes. Leave her as much room for manoeuvre as possible.

Encouraging your child to meet the standards and obey the rules

● Be prepared for a lot of hard work, especially at the beginning. Often it is far easier to give up the struggle and do things yourself. Remember that you are laying the foundation for your child's behaviour in the years ahead when you will not be there to 'make' her behave. Moreover, if you do the work early, you can prevent problems developing later. You may be able to ignore a pre-schooler who is aggressive, but what about an aggressive teenager?

- The better you know your child — her likes and dislikes, her needs and desires — the more chance you have of getting her to behave well.

- When you ask your child to do what you say, make your requests specific, so that she knows exactly what is required of her. Asking a child to tidy her toys is too vague; her idea of a tidy set of toys may be quite different from yours. Instead, ask her to put her toys in the toy-box. For younger children, you may need to limit the request and be very specific: 'You put Dolly and Teddy in the toy-box and I will pick up all the bricks.' Gradually you can make her tasks more challenging, all the time keeping pace with her abilities.

  Make only one request at a time. If you want her to get ready to go out, say: 'You must stop playing now, we are going out.' Only when she has complied with that request do you make the next one: 'Now, why don't you put on your anorak', and so on to the next request. If you issue a string of orders like 'Come on now, stop playing, get your clothes on, don't forget your boots and your hat . . . where are your mittens? . . . I said put away your toys . . .', your child may get confused, do things in the wrong order and also feel resentful.

- State your requests clearly and speak directly to your child. Do not issue a request over your shoulder as you rush past. Get her attention by calling her name and looking at her. Many children do not do as they are asked because they do not hear their parents' requests, being too absorbed in play. If you are not sure whether your child has heard you, ask her if she did. Do this gently. After all, the purpose is to find out if she has heard you, not to issue a warning. For really serious requests, to do with her safety, ask your daughter to repeat your instruction.

- Try to reach a point where you have to state a request only once, at least for some of the time. Young children are heedless, so a certain amount of repetition is essential. However, if you get into the habit of constantly repeating yourself, your child will conclude, sensibly, that your first request can be ignored and that she can safely wait until you say it for the fifth time before she needs to take notice.

- Increase the chances of her doing what you want the first time by making sure that you have her attention and by good timing. It is not a good idea to issue a request when your child is engrossed in play or frustrated by something. If you can, wait until she is more receptive. Remember that the idea is actually to get her to do as you ask, not to demand instant obedience.

- Give your child time to do as you ask. It may take her some seconds to register your request and get organised to do it. Watch how long it actually takes her and allow for that time in future. Giving her sufficient time will mean that if she actually does as you ask, she will feel that she has done so willingly and you can praise her for that. On the other hand, if you make a request and right afterwards issue an order or a threat, your child will feel compelled to comply (or resist), and then what can you praise?

- Develop a special way of ensuring immediate compliance in emergencies and make sure that she knows what this is. If you normally talk in an ordinary tone of voice to your child, you will find that if you shout out a loud 'No!' or 'Stop!' you will stop her in her tracks. This is a vital signal to have in dangerous situations, for example, if you see her about to step out in front of a car or touch a hot saucepan. If you shout and roar about everything, how will you signal that *this* time it is really serious?

- Respond immediately with praise when your child does as you ask. You can thank her while she is actually doing what you asked or immediately afterwards. Follow the guidelines in 'The Second Year' for praising and giving attention.

- Start early and start modestly in helping your child to do as you ask. It is easier to get children to co-operate in major things if they have had experience of obliging from an early age. Even very young children can put their toothbrush back in the holder or their pyjamas under the pillow. Begin by making only one or two requests a day, allowing yourself ample time to follow up on them.

If bedtime is a problem, start by saying: 'Let's go upstairs to bed now.' She may still argue and dilly-dally upstairs as you get her undressed, but concentrate on getting her simply to go upstairs. Once she consistently complies with that first request, add another, like asking her to take off her shoes. Once more, wait until she does this consistently and reliably, then move on to her tights, and wait again. Them move on to the rest of her clothing, brushing her teeth, and so on. Your goal is to get her to be able to respond to the more complex request of 'Now it's time for you to go up and get ready for bed'.

- Focus on the task in hand. If your child protests about going to bed, you can say firmly but gently 'I'll talk about that when you are upstairs'. In other words, you keep all your attention and hers on getting the first, small task done. Then you can chat, let her tell why she thinks you are being unreasonable, read her a story or whatever else she wants.

- Tell her simply why you are asking her to do something. If you want her to tidy her toys, you can explain that toys do not get broken if they are organised/she can find them when she is in a hurry/toys like their own 'special bed' just as she does/she will not trip on them and hurt herself, and so on. That way, she gradually learns why there is a rule about tidiness and can apply it to other situations.

- Allow your child to disagree with you. If she argues convincingly against one of your requests, you can change your mind. That way, she learns that reasoned argument and discussion sometimes can work. If you half-accept her point, but still see some merit in your request, negotiate and compromise. That way she will learn that everybody has rights and the best solution is one that takes into account all these rights. You will be relieved if she has learned that lesson well by the time she is a teenager. If you are not convinced by her argument, you can allow her to disagree, but still insist on her doing as you ask. That way she learns that there are limits.

● If you expect especially good behaviour in certain situations, you should explain the special rules beforehand. By telling your child ahead of time, you create the expectation of good behaviour. Give her a role to play in the situation. In the supermarket she can help you find and pack items of shopping. During a social visit, if she is shy, you can help her to chat by asking her to talk about something that happened to her recently. If she is very talkative, you can help her to stay quiet, while you chat, by bringing along a book or toy for her.

Keep trips short at the beginning. Fifteen minutes shopping or ten minutes visiting a neighbour are a good start. If you have to be there for longer, it is better to go alone or to bring another adult because younger pre-school children, up to about age three-and-a-half, soon come to the limit of their good behaviour. You can increase the length and frequency of these visits as your child learns to obey the special rules.

Punishment

The most powerful punishment for your child is your disapproval. Inevitably, you will sometimes feel irritated, even angry, and disappointed with her behaviour. Do not underestimate the effect this has on her and on her self-esteem. The wise parent will try to keep disapproval to a minimum. The more important task is to teach your child how to behave, not to react negatively to what she has just done. If you are angry, make sure she knows it is her behaviour, not herself, of which you disapprove.

When your child fails to meet her own standards or to please you she feels disappointed. Pre-school children are prone to guilt. That, in itself, is sufficient punishment. Again, the wise parent tries to minimise the occasions when this is likely to happen.

Much of what you are trying to teach your child is for her own good. You are trying to protect her from the consequences of not being competent, independent or of being anti-social. If, after all your efforts and warnings, she persists in behaving badly, she will suffer 'punishment' from the world outside the family. If she will not play by the rules of a game and cheats, or if she is unpleasant to her friends, she will not be a favoured playmate. If she smashes her toy in temper, afterwards she will be very upset by the effects of her own anger. That will be punishment enough. Your role then will be to offer sympathy and good advice to a receptive, sadder but wiser little girl.

Occasionally your child may behave in a way you find intolerable. Usually at this age, this is not serious misbehaviour. More likely, she is temporarily out of control. This very often happens when her ordinary routine is broken and a high level of frustration or excitement has built up. Christmas, birthdays, a house full of visitors, a long and tiring journey or shopping trip, all can lead to a build-up of tension. Punishment is not the answer here. Rather, your task is to contain the build-up of tension and remove her. You may need to stay with a very young or very upset child until she calms down. You can put an older child in a quiet room, preferably not her bedroom, because you do not want her to associate unpleasant events with going to sleep. Keep the child under discreet supervision so that she does not harm herself. Five minutes on her own is usually enough.

As your child gets older, serious misbehaviour can be punished by depriving her of ordinary privileges, watching TV for instance. Make sure you follow through with your threat to withdraw a privilege. Do it immediately after the misbehaviour, but be sure that your child knew what was required of her and that she got due warning. Most important, do not overuse this technique. Once you see how effective it is, it is tempting to use it to stop minor misbehaviour. All that will happen is that it will lose its effectiveness for the times you really need to impose it.

Physical punishment may help you let off steam and clear the air, but that is all. It may also succeed in stopping misbehaviour immediately, but it will interfere with your child's progress in developing self-control. The effect of physical punishment is to concentrate your child's attention on not getting caught instead of on resisting temptation, which is the basis of self-control.

The other problem is that children do not remember why they were smacked. What they remember is the pain and the anger. A lot of physical punishment builds up frustration in children, frustration that shows up in aggressive behaviour to their friends, and eventually to their parents. Physical punishment feeds on itself. Most cases of serious child abuse start as attempts at discipline that go horribly wrong.

Special treats

Many parents are wary of this technique, and rightly so. Children do not need to be bribed to do things if they already want to please their parents by being good, as most children do. But offering special treats sensibly has a valuable role in teaching your child to behave. We give treats to our children all the time and are hardly aware of it. Examples of effective special treats include spending extra playtime with you, extra television time, choice of television programme, playing with an especially loud or messy toy, or trips to places your child particularly likes.

The idea is to become more aware of the 'naturally occurring' treats in your daily relationship with your child. Next, you try occasionally to associate some of these with the good behaviour you want to encourage in your child. This technique is a useful incentive when your child has to do something demanding. It would be manipulation and an unfair exercise of power only to give her treats when she is exceptionally well-behaved. You should continue to give your child all the good things in life as you always have, simply because you love her and want to see her happy.

Parents are usually generous and self-sacrificing with their children, but it is sensible to make a positive connection between your good behaviour and their good behaviour. Very often we give children special treats and then feel disappointed because they behave badly. So we nag and needle them for not being grateful.

If you want your child to co-operate, you can say, 'Now, we'll play your favourite game because you helped me set the table.' This is much better than to play the game without asking her to help, and then feel full of resentment at how ungrateful and selfish she is because she would not help.

Guidelines for using special treats:

● State clearly what behaviour you are rewarding. For example, say, 'Now I'm going to read you a special story because you waited quietly for me to finish talking on the phone.'

● Double the positive effect by praising her as well. Do not just give her something with the attitude of 'off you go now, you've got enough out of me'. To be effective, *special treats must make your child feel good about herself.*

● Give the special treat only after or during the good behaviour. Never give it in return for a promise of good behaviour. Your child may forget or change her mind or not really understand what a promise means. Then you will feel resentful.

● Special treats work only if you award things your child likes, rather than what you think she should like. If you are not sure what she regards as a special treat, ask her.

● Do not give special treats of which you disapprove, and do not use a late bedtime as a special treat if you are trying to encourage her to go to bed at a regular hour.

● Match the special treat to how important and difficult the child's task is. If she is a restless and impulsive child, learning to wait patiently is very hard for her and merits a special treat.

● Do not use special treats to stop misbehaviour, because your child will try to get another one by repeating the misbehaviour.

Maintaining your child's self-esteem

Most parents feel affectionate and proud when their children achieve something, but it is essential to express these feelings directly. Many adults with low self-esteem remember no direct expressions of affection and praise from their parents. As children they had to rely on eavesdropping in the hope of hearing good things being said about them. So, never hesitate to express your good feelings about your child's accomplishments.

On the other hand, when your child has a shortcoming, treat it as something that she herself can overcome. For example, say, 'I know you are disappointed that you did not get that right. Never mind. Next time, if you spend more time at it/try harder/do it when you are not tired, you will do much better.' Your child gradually will come to share your confidence in her abilities and will feel optimistic and in control.

When your child is caught doing something forbidden, usually she will become distressed. In that case, make her realise that she is upset because she was doing wrong, not because she is afraid of punishment. Say, for example: 'You are crying now because you know you did a bad thing. I know you want to be a good girl, and this is what happens, you get really upset when you are not being a good girl.'

Explain why you want her to behave in a particular way. Say, for example, 'We don't hit other people. If you hit Mary, she will not want to play with you. Then you will be sad', rather than simply assert 'Stop that!'

Help your child to see things from other people's point of view. Express your disapproval and disappointment when she causes someone distress. This is more effective if you do it with feeling. Draw her attention firmly to how the other person is feeling. Suggest ways in which she can relieve the person's distress. 'Now look what you have done. Katie is upset because you pushed her and she fell and hurt her hand. Go and say "Sorry, Katie". Maybe she would like you to kiss her sore hand. Then she'll feel better.' Such appeals are effective only if your child knows that you take her own feelings seriously.

Conclusion

By the time you bring your child to the gates of primary school, you have helped her through her most important and formative years. All the hard work you have put in will now be evident in her accomplishments and independence. You have also equipped her with skills and qualities that will hibernate inside her until she needs to use them in the years ahead, when she is facing the challenges and temptations of adolescence and adulthood. For the moment, you are facing the calmer seas of the school years, when your child will think that, as parents go, you could not be much better. Relish the calm as long as it lasts!

Children bring up their parents as much as their parents bring them up. For most of us, parenting is a rather hit-and-miss affair. We muddle through, with only our own rearing to guide us. What I have tried to do is offer the kind of practical advice that will enable you to take a confident step forward. I will have succeeded if any of this information makes it easier for you to remember how it is to be a child, and makes it more enjoyable for you to be a parent.

Middle childhood (age 6-12)

Andy Conway

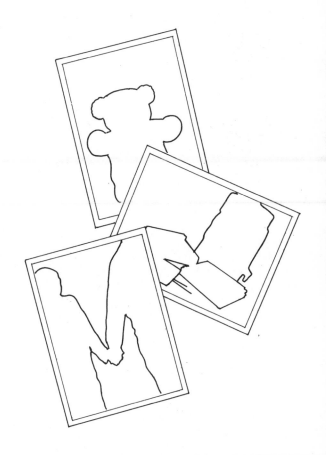

Middle childhood (age 6-12)

Parents perhaps best remember their middle childhood as their primary school years. Can you remember your primary school years? Where you lived? Your old primary school? Is it still there? Do you remember your teachers with fondness or otherwise? Can you remember your first day in primary school? Who brought you to school on that day? Do you remember those long summer holidays and the things you did? During those years your parents also matured and progressed through seven years of married life. These were very important years for you and there is no doubt that the middle years of your own child will mark another important phase in his development.

Throughout the years from six to twelve, children build on their early childhood experiences and continue to make great strides in their development. In the first five years major tasks were achieved, such as walking, talking and toilet-training. The tasks of middle childhood are less obvious to us as parents, although we become preoccupied with our children's schooling and are concerned that they should learn to read, write, spell, do arithmetic and be on the whole good pupils. We also wish our children to behave well and not to let themselves and us down in the playground, in the classroom, on the street, in church or in any other social situation. We also want our children to be good at home and expect them, by and large, to follow our rules and directions and cause us as little worry as possible.

It is often said that our childhood years are the happiest years of our life. Do you agree? How were your childhood years?

How would you rate the quality of your six-to-twelve-year olds' lives? Growing up is never easy and is not without its weekly difficulties, that will require your full attention as parents. From birth, children grow gradually towards independence. This growing towards independence in our human species is a long, sometimes unpredictable but yet inevitable process.

Between age six and twelve, our children's social world is continually expanding. When a child of five enters primary school, he enters a new world of experience. These days children are well-prepared for their new school because they have already attended a playgroup or pre-school. Children starting primary school now are generally better able to behave themselves in class. They know that listening to teacher is important and are able to respond to the instructions of another adult who is not their parent. The world of primary school introduces the child to a wide circle of friends and to the busy learning opportunities in junior infants.

As our children progress through each year in the middle years, their personality becomes more noticeable and distinct. For example, a seven-year-old will tend to take much more care than a six-year-old when playing a game. Six-year-olds can be rough in their play, tend to be rowdy and often leave their bedrooms and playrooms in a mess. The seven-year-old is more concerned to obey the rules and tends both to play and work hard.

Even after a long day in school, many eight-year-olds are still energetic and are looking for something else to do. They are more methodical in their approach to games and will enjoy being the leader of a group. The eight-year-old is better able to explain how he feels and is usually more willing to express his thoughts. He is also more anxious to help with the day-to-day affairs of the house.

By age nine the child is beginning to show even more independence. A nine-year-old is capable of looking at himself critically and shows greater confidence in his own world. Perhaps he will insist on going to school on his own, and he can become very aware of how other nine-year-olds regard him. A nine-year-old will begin to show more concern about family matters and he will become worried if all is not running well in his family. He will also feel responsible for his younger brothers and sisters and if one of them misbehaves in school or in a social gathering, he will feel embarrassed and will try to correct them. Many parents find that children take up quite intense interests when they are nine. These can become the basis for hobbies, such as photography or stamp collecting, which will last for many years. The success of these hobbies often depends on the amount of encouragement, interest and support that parents give the child.

It appears that, at about age nine, marked differences occur between boys and girls. They usually like to play with children of their own sex and will be interested in different activities. When boys and girls of nine are together, they tease one another, jokingly link each other in future marriages and generally become giggly and boisterous. In general, the nine-year-old is a reasonable if inexperienced youngster.

In their tenth and eleventh years, children become more self-conscious and egocentric. At this age they like talking about themselves, enjoy expressing and comparing their views and are beginning to see themselves more objectively. They are able to make thoughtful observations on their own behaviour. There is an increased awareness of competition and comparison among ten- and eleven-year-olds. As the child progresses into his twelfth year, he gains more freedom and responsibilities because his parents accept his growing maturity.

Throughout these middle years we, as parents, are also learning and maturing. We are becoming more assured in the rearing of our children and will have benefited from the accumulated years of experience — seven days a week, twenty-four hours a day. This probably is the only training we get to be parents — on the job — so it is amazing how well we do. Parenting often is a case of trial and error, although much more information about child development has been available to us in the last twenty years. We tend to draw on our own experiences as children, though quite often we try to rear our children differently to the way we think we were reared. This often creates difficulties.

When our children are in their 'middle years', we tend to be frantically busy between eight and nine in the morning and again from three to eight in the evening. Our children usually go to bed by 8.30 or 9.00 pm and sleep soundly. Of course, some will have nightmares, but generally we can relax in the knowledge that they are exhausted after a very busy day and are sleeping soundly.

Problems

All normal children of six to twelve experience a wide variety of common problems in their day-to-day lives. Sometimes these are frightening and serious and may lead parents to seek professional advice or help. However, we should not forget that commonsense will be our best guide to most childhood problems. Nearly all of them are easy to overcome, but we must take stock and tackle them methodically. Many of these problems are essentially home-based, although the child may have problems to do with school. Sometimes the difficulties may arise in both the home and the school. We shall now look in more detail at a selection of common difficulties that occur in both the home and the school. I shall describe the nature of these problems, possible reasons for them, and shall offer practical suggestions for overcoming them.

Common problems at home

1. *Problems of conduct*

Throughout their development all children present a wide range of normal behavioural difficulties. There is no such thing as a perfect child, and we must recognise that all children's behaviour serves some purpose. Can you think of reasons why your child occasionally misbehaves? For example, when you say to your son that it is now time to go to bed and he responds by whining, pleading, or continuing to watch television, what he is doing is obvious. Your child wants to be in control. He wants to dictate what he should do and, by being difficult, hopes that he will bully you into giving in and saying 'OK you can stay up for twenty more minutes.'

Such conduct is designed to test us. Children attempt to try our patience and authority in order to get their own way. We often overreact, raising our voices, sometimes becoming abusive and, if our instructions are not followed, we can even smack our children. Do you agree that such things are not uncommon in your home?

Children will baulk at a wide variety of commonplace

parental requests. In the mornings before school, parents easily can become exasporated because their children are slow to get dressed, have breakfast, brush their teeth and so on. Similarly, the tasks after school — changing out of school uniforms, helping around the house, doing homework, having supper and going to bed — can lead to rows if children dig in their heels.

An important word to keep in mind is *obedience*. To enable the house to run smoothly, children must learn to obey. Once it has been established as routine, obedience gives children a sense of discipline and order and can make them feel in control of their lives. Children get more satisfaction from being good than from being disobedient. If they persist in disobeying us, it is fair to say that we as parents may have mismanaged the situation.

If you think your child is being persistently disobedient, the first step is to sit down with your partner and discuss what this problem is. For example, you may be having difficulty getting your child to do her homework. When you have identified the exact problem, decide what the ideal solution should be. You may decide that your child should do her homework between five and six o'clock. Choose the room and table where she is to work. Decide what the circumstances will be. For instance, the television, radio and record-player will be switched off, there will be adequate lighting and table space. Record your ideal plan on a sheet of paper.

You may wish to consider the bedtime routine. What time do you want your child to be in bed, with stories read and lights out? If you want her to be in bed by 8.30, at what time do you ask her to get ready for bed? Be specific. Plan what the tasks of preparing for bed are: changing into pyjamas, pre-bedtime snacks, brushing teeth. Having worked out this ideal model with your partner, make sure that you both are happy to implement the plan and that you are not going to deviate from it. It is vital in helping children to be disciplined that both parents show a similar discipline and do not contradict each other.

The next phase is to speak to your child about what you have decided. Be relaxed, speak slowly and clearly and show warmth and affection. Invite your child to comment on what you have decided. Explain what the new arrangement is going to be and be sure that your child is left in no doubt about what you both expect of her. If you wish, you could start a chart system, so that there is a visible record of how the programme is going. A wall chart can be put in the kitchen and, on the successful completion of her homework, your child can be given a star; on managing to get herself settled in bed by the appointed time, she may get another star. If you decide that your child does not deserve a star, then you leave a blank. At the end of each week the child's behaviour can be reviewed and each star can be linked to a small reward. Such a programme can be discontinued when the child has established a pattern. Once the pattern has been set, continue to praise your child. It is important to let children know that you appreciate what they are doing and like them for it. The above methods will help your child to understand what is required of her and to know that by being disciplined and obedient, she will feel good. The above model can be adapted to a wide variety of behavioural problems in the home.

Choosing appropriate rewards and punishments for misbehaviour is a further important aspect. It is well known that if we want to increase the occurrence of good behaviour, we should praise our children when they behave well, and when we see behaviour we do not like, it is important to have a way of ensuring that it does not reoccur. One of the best methods is to let your child know that you do not like what he is doing and that you are displeased by what has occurred. You also may decide to deprive your child of television, treats or trips, because of misbehaviour, but you must know exactly what you wish to achieve if you are to withdraw favours. If you are depriving the child of treats, you should deprive him on the day of the misdemeanour and not days later.

When we consider punishment, we may think of the notion of smacking, slapping or hitting our children. There is little doubt that a disobedient child will respond very quickly to a slap, but commonsense tells us that the slap usually has only a short-term effect and does not lead to a change of behaviour or to the child becoming more obedient. Indeed, when we hit our child, we offer him a model of aggression and unfairly take advantage of our strength. Sometimes children are badly hurt when adults set about them.

2. *Bedwetting*

Bedwetting is a fairly common and sometimes distressing problem that can affect children between the ages of six and twelve years. Usually the child wets the bed at night while he is asleep. This is an important factor because he really has no control over what happens. Most children gain full control of their bladders by the fourth year. Others will have occasional accidents up to the sixth or seventh year, but then will gain full control. A small percentage of children will continue to wet the bed even into their teenage years. Yet another group of children will have been fully trained by four but suddenly, at the age of eight to ten, they revert to wetting the bed.

Parents whose child is wetting the bed should consider the following question: Has my child ever been fully dry at night?

If your answer to this question is 'no', then it is most likely that your child's bladder and its wiring system is not yet fully operational. However, you can help your child to control his bladder.

If the answer to the question is 'yes', then your child has gained full bladder control but has lost it temporarily. When did your child achieve bladder control? When did he lose it? How many years has he shown himself to be fully in control of his bladder with no instances of bedwetting? First, discuss the matter with your family doctor because the child may have a physical problem, such as an infection. If it is not a medical problem, you can assume that the bedwetting is a reaction to stress of some kind.

How to help a child who wets the bed

Have you decided which type of bedwetting your child has? Let us now look at a child who is perhaps eight years of age but who has not yet achieved full bladder control at night. How have you been coping with this so far? Many parents find bedwetting difficult to deal with. You probably have tried many ways of overcoming the problem, and may well have become so frustrated that you have spoken harshly to your child. Mothers, in particular, may be fed up with having constantly to launder soiled sheets.

It is time to start afresh. Accept that it is not your child's or your fault. His bladder will 'grow up' in time and you are going to start today to help him. It is important to explain to him how the kidneys and bladder work. Tell him that the bladder is merely a bag or balloon that collects waste products which result when the kidneys cleanse the blood. Ask your child to think of and remember the feeling of fullness in his bladder. Have him understand what it means to be 'bursting' or 'dying to go to the toilet'. If he can recognise this feeling, you are helping him to identify the powerful signals that are being sent from his bladder to his brain, telling him that he is full and that he must go to the toilet. It is important not to make the child anxious or upset about his problem but to deal with it in an open and positive way. You might ask him one day to hold out for as long as possible before he goes to the toilet. For example, you could ask him to empty his bladder before he leaves for school and then not to use the toilet again until after his second school break. This will help his bladder control and will train him to recognise and control the signals his brain receives and transmits. This learning eventually will become effective in controlling the bladder while he is asleep.

At night you can lift your child before you go to bed. This will help him get into the habit of emptying his bladder and may prevent a wet bed. Not taking drinks in the evenings has proved to be of little help. Restricting a child's drinks may also induce anxiety which could compound the problem. You could put up a chart, listing the days of the week, to help. If on Wednesday night your child has a dry bed, then in the space under Wednesday you can insert a star or a smiling face. If the bed is wet, you can choose to insert nothing or you can draw a cloud releasing rain. The achievement of stars can be linked to some agreed reward. You might decide not to reward single-night successes but to agree with your child that three consecutive dry nights will earn a reward. Adopting such a programme often can help your child to achieve full bladder control.

Another method is a pad and buzzer system, which you can buy or obtain from your local public health nurse. Your child sleeps on a urine sensitive pad, made in such a way that when he begins to wet the bed, it activates a buzzer loud enough to wake him. Agree with him that he will go to the toilet and empty his bladder as soon as he is awakened. One disadvantage of this method is that the whole house tends to be woken up by the alarm, although a personalised earphone is available.

If your child has been dry at night for some years and suddenly starts to wet the bed again, then you should find out if something is worrying him. How has school been going? Is he suddenly having difficulty with his teacher? Has homework become harder, so that he is beginning to doubt his ability? Is your child being bullied at school? Have there been recent stresses in your family, such as financial difficulties, health problems, or marital tensions? Have you moved house or has your child changed schools? Has he suffered any recent trauma, such as a road traffic accident, or has he witnessed something upsetting? Have you had a baby recently? Has there been a death in either parent's family or extended family? These are important questions and you should think carefully about them. It should be possible to pinpoint the source of your child's anxiety. When you have identified it, you should talk to him about it and take any steps necessary to ensure that he can get over his worries.

If he says that he is being bullied in school and is nervous about going there, you must visit the school and try to resolve things. When you help your child to understand and cope with his particular anxiety, he will regain normal bladder control.

The child who refuses to go to school

All children are afraid of something; fear of the dark, of strangers, and of animals are common fears in childhood. Sometimes these fears last for a comparatively short time. At other times they can create serious worries for the child and her parents.

It is important to distinguish between a fear and a phobia. Your child may dislike dogs and may feel uneasy when she sees one approaching. This is a fear. But if your child is anxious about the prospect of meeting a dog on the street and refuses to walk to school in order not to meet one, then your child has a phobia.

When a child develops school phobia, she refuses point-blank to attend school. Some children pretend to leave for school and then 'mitch' by going elsewhere. It is important to distinguish between mitching and school refusal. In the latter, the child stays at home with one or other parent. At all times the parents know where the child is.

The parents of a child who refuses to go to school usually
do not know why. The teacher and school principal normally
will also be at a loss. The child may complain that she is scared
of her teacher or the other pupils. Some children may say that
they do not know why they are frightened. When the child
is at home, she is happy and shows no sign of worry, but if
she is forced to go to school, she becomes miserable and will
try to run home. If she is forced to stay in school, she may
become angry and abusive and may even panic. The child can
put herself at risk if she becomes very upset — for example
by running tearfully from school onto a busy roadway.

By and large, children who refuse to go to school do not
have learning difficulties and are normally well-behaved pupils.
This refusal to go to school usually occurs unexpectedly,
although sometimes it can be a gradual resistance.

In order to understand the nature of the child's suffering,
we need to look at how anxiety affects us all. Anxiety is part
of the human condition; it can keep us alert, motivated and
generally able to cope with demanding situations. We become
more aware of our anxiety before an important examination,
an interview, or a visit to the bank manager. Imagine the
following scene. You are walking home alone late at night.
It is dark and cold. Suddenly you hear footsteps behind you
and you immediately become apprehensive. Your anxiety
instantly manifests itself in four ways:

1. Physical. Your heart beats faster and you breathe more
   quickly. You may feel yourself becoming cold, shivery and
   sweaty; you may have a sudden urge to go to the toilet. Your
   eyes and ears become ultra alert, and your brain, lungs and
   major muscles receive a huge increase in blood supply. You
   are ready for fight or flight.

2. Thoughts. Your head is suddenly spinning with questions.
   Who might it be? You tell yourself that something dreadful
   could be about to happen to you. You think about the recent
   increase in crime and what you intend to do if you are
   attacked.

3. Behaviour. Your behaviour changes. Before hearing the

footsteps you were walking leisurely home. Now you may walk much faster and perhaps even break into a trot.

4. Feeling. You were relaxed and in a good mood. Now you are scared, and upset.

Children and adults are capable of experiencing these four aspects in frightening situations. When children or adults develop a phobia, they will have experienced anxiety for some time before. A phobia is a bad or faulty cure for anxiety. When a phobia develops, our anxiety occurs only when we are in the presence of the feared object. Agoraphobia is a fear of open spaces. If those who suffer from this phobia avoid open spaces, they do not feel anxious. If a child has school phobia, not going there will help her to control her anxiety.

There is little doubt that a child who refuses to go to school is suffering from anxiety. In nearly all cases, the source of the child's anxiety is fear of separation from the mother. Indeed, many people contend that the term 'school phobia' is misleading because the child's greatest fear is leaving the mother. These children fear that something terrible will happen to their mother if they are not with her.

The child who refuses to go to school usually makes vague complaints about it. She may protest about going or may absolutely refuse to go. Sometimes those who attend school, go under protest and have to be coerced and manipulated by their teachers, parents and even by the school principal. While there, they are tense and preoccupied. In the child's family there will nearly always have been a serious illness, a move of house, the loss of a relative, or any similar stressful circumstance.

John is a ten-year-old boy whom I saw some years ago. He gradually had become afraid to attend school and was referred to our clinic. Discussions with John's family revealed that his mother had been to various hospitals to find the explanation of certain physical symptoms she was experiencing. In spite of reassurances from a series of consultants, she was convinced that she was seriously and perhaps terminally ill. She had made arrangements for the family's future after her death.

Although John's mother believed that she could conceal her anxiety and fear of death from her easygoing husband and children, she did not hide it from John. He was acutely aware of her worry and suddenly found it unbearable to be away from her because he expected something dreadful to happen to her in his absence. Throughout his childhood he had been very close to his mother and particularly dependent on her; he liked to come into her bed at night. He had difficulty starting playschool and was very upset for a number of months before he eventually settled down.

In another family, Ann, aged nine, refused suddenly and obstinately to attend school. Her grandmother had died a week before. The family had attended the funeral and Ann's mother had looked after her mother's personal affairs quickly and efficiently. The family did not discuss the grandmother's death in any detail and tried to get on with their lives. One morning, as Ann's mother was getting the children off to school, Ann flatly refused to go. It transpired that she had been thinking about the death of her grandmother, about death and loss, and about the possibility of her parents dying. She had not discussed her fears with her parents. Ann's fear that her mother might die made it essential that she be with her to assure herself that her mother was alive and well.

It is clear that both John and Ann suffered extreme anxiety. In both cases their parents were not aware of the degree of their child's anxiety. The talks with both families were aimed at improving relationships and patterns of communication and establishing ways of dealing with the stresses that the families were experiencing. It was vital to explore the nature of John's mother's imagined illness. Ann's family had to look at the mourning of her grandmother. Ann's mother had refused to acknowledge that her mother was dead. In both families it was thought important for the father to play a more assertive role and for the father–child relationship to be strengthened.

What to do if your child refuses to go to school

If a child refuses to attend school, both parents should examine recent family events carefully. Your child's refusal indicates that she is suffering from anxiety. The source of this anxiety is probably a fear of separating from her mother. This fear, normal in young children, has resurfaced because of a family illness, death or stress. Both parents must identify the reasons for their child's anxiety. If they think they know, they should discuss the problem with the child and help her to understand why she is feeling anxious. The parents should explain what it is to be anxious and should help their child to understand the four different ways in which anxiety affects us. You must be firm about school and insist that your daughter return immediately. The longer the child remains out of school, the more difficult it will be to get her back.

Making sure that your child goes back to school will mean a meeting with her teacher and the school principal. Draw up a careful programme that will enable your child to return to school with the least amount of difficulty. She should be fully involved in the drawing up of any programme. Some children respond very quickly once the source of their anxiety has been determined, and they may agree to return to school full-time. A system of rewards may be implemented; these rewards will be given at the end of an agreed period.

If a child is very anxious, it may be necessary to have her return to school on a phased basis. For example, in the first week the child may be asked to go to school for an hour a day only. During the first week, the child perhaps may go to the principal's office for this hour. In the second week, the child may be transferred to the classroom for an hour, and the period of time she spends in school can be gradually extended as the weeks progress. This phased approach allows for the gradual reduction of her anxiety.

In all situations where a child is suffering from school refusal, it is important for fathers to help overcome the problem in a strong and positive fashion. The father must spend a fair amount of time with the child in the evenings and at weekends. If this strategy does not work, the father should seek professional help and guidance.

The concept of self-esteem

As your child moves through primary school, he develops a wide range of social and personal skills. These skills are drawn on daily within his family, school and among his friends. They will help him to express what he is feeling in most situations. The child learns to put across his point of view and to listen to and understand the other person's point of view. If he has good social skills, he can successfully cope with most tricky situations and better manage the demands of day-to-day life.

When he copes well in varied social settings, he feels good and this enhances his self-esteem.

Self-esteem is an important aspect of our personality. How do you feel about yourself? Do you feel that your views and opinions are respected? Are you popular? Do other people respect and value you? Do you feel that you are handling your life competently? Your level of self-esteem as a parent has been determined by various stages of life through which you have passed. Loss of self-esteem, or a poorly developed sense of self-worth, can make us ineffective in our personal and social lives. It is important that, as parents, we understand what we must do to help our children develop a positive and strong sense of their own selves.

Self-esteem may be compared to water — a vital life resource. Imagine that your child is born with an empty barrel. Your task is to fill this barrel with self-esteem so that by the time he reaches maturity, he has a full barrel and a strong sense of self-worth. Each time you praise your child, cuddle him, smile at him, each time you bestow your approval on your child, you add a cup of water to his barrel. On the other hand, if you are uncomplimentary, negative, and dismissive of things in which he is keenly interested, you are taking cups of water from his barrel.

Acting-out/Acting-in behaviour

When our children are having difficulties, they may 'act out' or 'act in'. To illustrate, let us look at our own lives. If you are having trouble with a troublesome neighbour, you may find that you are unable to cope and may adopt an acting-out response or an acting-in response. In the former, you may verbally abuse your neighbour, send him threatening letters, bang on his door or throw things into his garden. Here you are acting out your frustration, letting your neighbour know that you are not pleased. Now you will agree that this is not a logical way of dealing with the problem.

You perhaps may act in in response to the problem, sitting and brooding in your house, drinking endless cups of coffee and not going out in case you may run into your neighbour. You also feel helpless and despondent.

Children adopt similar responses when they find themselves

in distressing or difficult situations. Nearly all six- to twelve-year-olds go through phases when they feel hard done by and unloved. The source of the child's unhappiness or worry can be something at home or at school. For example, a child who is being bullied in school can suffer an emotional crisis. A child can feel unloved or rejected by his family. If either parent is depressed or if the couple are going through a bad patch in their marriage, the child can feel very upset but will not know how to cope. The child wrongly may suspect that he is the source of the difficulties and can feel guilty and even blame himself. In many such situations the child will possess the skills to tell his parents how he is feeling and will be able to help his parents come to a solution. However, those children who do not have these resources may show their unhappiness and confusion by 'acting out' or 'acting in'.

Children's most common forms of acting-out behaviour include stealing, lying, fighting, the destruction of property, the breaking of parental rules, and other techniques for gaining attention. If you think your child is behaving in this way, you must understand that the behaviour is occurring because of some inner need. For example, a ten-year-old boy may keep stealing his father's money, cigarette lighter, or other personal possessions. He may hide them in his own bedroom but invariably one of his parents will find them. Perhaps the child is expressing his insecurity in his relationship with his father and he gains a sense of security from having his father's things in his room. It may be that he is setting himself up to be caught so that he can provoke his father into giving him more attention. Parents should not regard this form of stealing as criminal and should not brand their son as a thief.

All parents worry about juvenile delinquency and when we discover that our child is stealing we may jump to the conclusion that he is heading for a life of crime. The parents of a child who is 'acting out' must be concerned but careful not to apportion blame. They should talk with the child to find out how exactly he feels and to listen to his needs and wishes.

The most common forms of acting-in behaviours among primary school children include social withdrawal, depression and losing interest in activities that they once enjoyed. The reaction can vary from mild to severe; if it is mild, it often goes unnoticed. Teachers and parents frequently report that the acting-out child receives all the attention, while the acting-in child suffers in silence. Parents should be alert to this fact and if they think that their child is unusually withdrawn or depressed should try to find out why. Let your child know that you understand how he or she is feeling and help the child understand what is happening. Sometimes a mother herself may be going through a period of mild depression and the child's withdrawal may occur because she thinks she has lost her mother's attention and affection.

The child may also be worried about her mother not being well. It is commonly accepted that, when we become depressed, we lose interest in our day-to-day responsibilities and show a lack of enthusiasm for our parental role. As parents, we are of central importance in the development of our children's emotional life, and anything that lessens our capacities will have a considerable impact on our offspring.

Common learning problems at school

Self-expression, reading, spelling and writing are given a high priority within Ireland's primary school system. Over the past thirty years, in particular, parents have become more and more interested and concerned about their children's capacity to learn, reflecting the new society's demands for academic success. Young people today usually remain within the educational system until they are seventeen. Before the 1950s the majority of young people left school at fourteen and went out to work. Many of our older generation will acknowledge that there was far less emphasis on learning in their youth. Charles Dickens observed that children as young as eleven finished formal schooling and the boys ('little men') joined their fathers in his trade or career. The boys adopted their father's dress and went to work in the steel yards, the coalmines, or, like Dickens himself, in the blacking factory.

Today, in Ireland, teachers quickly recognise if a young child is finding it hard to learn to read. When parents hear this, they worry that their child's future educational progress may be impaired. For years, parents, teachers and psychologists have struggled with terms like 'dyslexia', 'congenital word blindness', 'backward readers' and 'specific learning disabilities'. Fortunately the educational system has responded remarkably well to children who have learning difficulties, and an array of support and remedial services are available to help overcome them.

The incidence of reading difficulties is difficult to assess, but it seems that at least one in every five children will have some form of learning difficulty. If you are concerned about your child's ability to read, it may be helpful to consider her difficulties in the context of the following five headings:

a) *Physical aspects*

Are you sure that your child's eyes and ears are functioning normally? All schools have periodic medical inspections and the school doctor almost certainly will spot if your child has a sensory defect. However, children are subject to ear infections and some may suffer a temporary loss of hearing. Observe your child's hearing ability. Does she like the television volume to be louder than the rest of the family? Does she sit very close to the television set? Has she a preferred ear with which she chooses to listen? Can she respond to low-voiced or whispered speech? Do you find that sometimes she does not follow your instructions or respond when you ask her to do something? The results of your observations will indicate whether you should arrange for your child to see an audiologist. If she squints her eyes while reading or writing, or if she brings her book close to her eyes, or complains that she has difficulty seeing, then you should have her eyesight tested.

How is your child's health? Learning is helped enormously if one is physically healthy. Does your child usually have a good night's sleep, so that when she arrives in school she is fresh, alert and able to concentrate. Ensure that your child has a nutritious breakfast that will set her up for the day ahead.

b) *Intellectual language abilities*

Are you happy that your child is of normal intelligence or do you consider that she may be a little slow intellectually? There is a positive link between intellectual ability and reading success, although some children, who are above average or even of superior, intelligence, find it very hard to learn to read.

Some children may not be ready for the programme that

is offered them in school. Junior infants and senior infants schools concentrate on the development of pre-reading skills.

In first and second class, learning to read becomes a much more formal and demanding matter. A child of weaker intelligence may begin to find it difficult to keep up with the programme. A skilful teacher will gear her programme to each child's intellectual level.

An important part of the child's intellectual capacity is her general level of language development. She must learn to be fluent in English and to speak clearly. The child must acquire a wide vocabulary and it is important to look at both her expressive and receptive language skills. Speech therapists distinguish between receptive and expressive language. As you read these sentences, you are using receptive language. You may not be able to talk, but if you are reading and understanding what is on the page, you are using receptive language skills. However, I know that if we could meet within the next few minutes, we could have a conversation in which you would express your views to me about what you have just read. This represents the expressive side of your language capacity.

Since children can show mixed abilities in these capacities, it is important to check that your child actually understands language correctly. Your child may also have a difficulty choosing the appropriate words to say what he wants to say. This shows that he has expressive problems. Many children who find it hard to learn to read will have expressive or receptive language difficulties. If so, a speech therapist should be asked to help.

c) *Social aspects*

A child lives within the social setting of a family. This family may or may not emphasise self-expression and communication. It is important that the child is encouraged to talk openly, to express her ideas, and to share her knowledge and experience with her parents. Does everyone in your family like to read? Do you speak of reading as a pleasurable pastime? Do you encourage your children to use reference books, encyclopaedias and dictionaries to improve their knowledge? Do you ask your children to write stories? Does the television set dominate more than it should in your house? Some children who come from homes where there is little emphasis on reading and exchanging thoughts will themselves experience reading difficulties.

d) *Emotional factors*

A ten-year-old child who is unhappy will have great difficulty applying himself within the formal setting of a classroom. Indeed, a child who is experiencing great difficulty with the school curriculum may develop low self-esteem. He may compare himself unfavourably with other pupils and begin to feel that he is not as good as they are. In spite of his efforts, he may find that he cannot keep up with the rest of the class. This makes him feel badly about himself and can further interfere with his learning.

e) *Perceptual factors*

Perception is greater than seeing or hearing. Human perceptual abilities are quite complex and elaborate information processing systems. Children may have perfect vision and hearing, but may have a significant visual or auditory perceptual difficulty. A common visual perceptual difficulty found in children is the tendency to reverse letters: 'b' is confused with 'd' and 'p' with 'q'. They may even reverse whole words and write 'saw' for 'was'. Some children experience difficulty associating sounds with letters. Asked to spell 'cat', some children will write 'cut'; 'sat' may become 'sit'.

Teaching methods

Teachers may use one particular method or a combination of several when teaching children to read. If you intend to help your child to develop his reading skills, you should consult his teacher about the method she uses. The 'look and say' or 'whole word' method aims to develop the child's sight vocabulary. Children are encouraged to see the words as whole patterns and to use their memory to develop their reading. The teacher may use flash cards to help children to learn words by sight. The card is shown to the child, who is told what the word is. The child then says the word and is encouraged to try to remember it. Gradually the number of flash cards presented to the child is increased and the child builds up a large sight vocabulary. Sometimes the cards contain a picture with the appropriate word printed underneath.

The 'sentence method' is an extension of the 'look and say' method. Here the child learns words in statements and sentences, for example 'Ann is in the garden.'

The phonic method of teaching reading focuses on the relationship between the sound and the letter. Having learnt the sound of the letters the child will analyse a word by breaking it up into its parts and by blending the sounds to make the whole word. Children may show a flair for any one, or indeed for all, the above methods and it is important to teach to the child's strengths rather than to his weakness.

If your child has a reading difficulty, consider the powerful influences that come to bear on his ability to learn. You may have some ideas about why your child is not progressing as well as he should. If so, speak to his teacher. Helpful suggestions can be shared and a programme can be agreed between the teacher and the parents. Many schools are lucky to have the services of a qualified remedial teacher who has the skills to assess a child's strengths and weaknesses and who can then begin a teaching programme with that child in a small group. A child who needs remedial teaching will be taken from his regular class for half-an-hour or more each day and will receive special teaching. Unfortunately, a large number of schools do not have the services of remedial teachers and many children suffer as a result.

A small number of children may find it difficult to learn because they have a weak intelligence. Such children are often described as being slow learners and have considerable problems with all forms of learning in the normal class. In many schools, particularly in the Dublin area, there are special classes to cater for the very slow pupil. On average these classes contain twelve to fourteen pupils. There are junior and senior levels. The programme is geared to the child's abilities and he is encouraged to perform to his capacity. It is often necessary to transfer a child to a special class when the demands of the normal curriculum prove to be beyond his abilities. Before this transfer can occur, you must talk to the school principal and the teacher. Your child will be referred to a psychologist for an assessment and, in consultation with the school, appropriate recommendations will be made.

A small number of children of average or even above average intellectual ability suffer learning difficulties. Often they come from normal home backgrounds. Such children frequently do not benefit from the usual remedial teaching. There are two schools in Dublin for such children: Catherine McAuley School in Baggot Street and Saint Oliver Plunkett's School in Monkstown. They adopt a special approach to children with specific learning disabilities and can make remarkable progress with them.

However, there will always be a small number of children who will continue to have problems with reading, spelling and writing throughout their lives, though it is important to recognise that the vast majority will establish and continue to build on an adequate level of literacy.

We have seen that children may have difficulties learning to read and spell because of specific language problems. In one Dublin school, there are two language classes where specialist teachers and speech therapists help the children to overcome their difficulties. The Association for Children and Adults with Learning Disabilities offers a comprehensive assessment and remedial service to individuals who are experiencing learning difficulties. The Association is at 27 Upper Mount Street, Dublin 2 and there are branches in Mullingar, Co. Westmeath and Newbridge, Co. Kildare.

Homework

The prescribed homework varies in quantity and quality depending on what stage your child is at in school. Homework is a vital extension into the home of the school curriculum. As a parent, you should talk to the class teacher about how homework should be done. Children must know what is required of them and also be aware that their parents are supporting them. It is necessary to agree a set time for homework and a regular place to do it. Ideally, the child should sit at a desk or a table with plenty of light and space. There should be no distractions such as television and radio, or other children who have no homework to do. Parents should supervise and answer questions, but should not do the actual work. The teacher will indicate the length of time the homework should take, but at primary school this is rarely more than an hour.

Homework can be stressful for parents and children alike. Many family rows flare up over homework and it is not uncommon for children to end up in tears and parents to feel frustrated. Homework should be a relaxed and enjoyable activity, but parents must recognise that learning is not easy and that homework tops the list of most children's least-liked activities outside school hours.

Bullying in school

In the average primary school hundreds of children gather every weekday. The school itself is a state organisation within which qualified teachers follow a prescribed curriculum which is designed so that each child may be enabled to realise his full potential. There is little doubt that the local national school is an extremely busy place. From the outside it is usually seen as an orderly, quiet and productive environment. Children busy themselves at maths, listen to stories, carry out projects, sing in unison and exercise in the gym and the playground.

Children are often loud, noisy and boisterous during play. They punch, trip and pummel one another. Children can have unhappy days in school. They are sometimes restless and inattentive and can be defiant and unwilling to co-operate. Teachers are skilled observers of child behaviour and can judge when to do something particular to help a child overcome his unhappiness.

Bullying is a widespread problem in many schools. Teachers, parents and the families of both the bully and the child who is being bullied all can suffer because of the bullying. Bullying is a subtle form of violence or intimidation. It is carried out by one child or by a group of children against another child, who usually is unable or afraid to defend himself.

Bullying can be: a) physical, where a child is punched and beaten, or psychological, where a child is threatened, warned or excluded; b) the intensity of the bullying can vary from horseplay and mild threats to vicious assault; c) a child may be bullied occasionally or continually. Unless it is checked, it can go on for months; d) most bullying is planned and carefully carried out. It is rarely accidental; e) the motivation for bullying varies. Boys who bully tend to do it to establish power and dominance. Girls tend to bully in order to exclude or intimidate the victim. In some schools, children have been bullied into bringing money and jewellery to their persecutors in order to avoid further punishment.

If your child is being bullied at school, he may be unwilling to discuss it with you. You may notice that he comes home without some of his belongings, but he will not tell you where they are. He may also come home with unaccounted-for cuts and bruises or perhaps his clothes are torn. Children who are being bullied may begin to wet the bed, may develop nervous tics, and may be afraid of going to school. They may complain of vague aches and pains and say that they are not liking school. Their school work may fall off and you may notice them beginning to struggle with their studies.

Some children are more vulnerable to bullying than others. The shy, reserved child is often picked on. The studious child who may be regarded as teacher's pet can also be set upon by a bully. Children who are of smaller stature than the rest of their class also become targets.

Bullies tend to have an enhanced sense of their own worth and often are stronger and more physically demanding than their victims. However, they may be bullying because of some deep-seated need within them. It is natural in any social system for an informal social order to emerge. Certain children in class will assume leadership roles and others will be more reserved. The bully may not like this social order and he will contrive to change things to suit his particular needs. He is certainly not the most popular boy or girl in the class and the brighter and more able students often will have sympathy for the bullied and resent the bully.

What to do if your child is being bullied

When you suspect that your child is being bullied, arrange a meeting with the school principal and class teacher. Explain that you have noticed signs that your child is being bullied or that he has told you about particular incidents of bullying. If bullying takes place within the school, it is largely the responsibility of the teaching staff to monitor and control it. Once the teachers are alerted to the fact that your child is being picked on, they should be able to stop it.

You can teach your child how to cope when he finds himself

in difficult situations. You can help him to be more assertive and encourage him to express his feelings. Many children may think that it is best to 'grin and bear it'. You should encourage your child to say 'no' and to be able to put forward reasons why he thinks the situation in which he finds himself is unfair.

Not all children find it easy to relax with their classmates. Much valuable work can be done at home and children can be trained how to relate to their brothers and sisters in a positive and effective manner. Indeed the home can become a rehearsal room within which children can practise the art of positive communication.

Teachers may be asked to discuss bullying in the classroom. If the subject is brought into the open, children can express their views about how bullying can be checked. The children can be asked to take part in a 'pretend' bullying scene, and a variety of ways to help beat the bully and the victim can be presented.

In serious cases of bullying, the school principal should speak to the bully's parents. This child needs help. Some parents will choose to remove their child from a school in which he is being bullied and transfer him to another school. This will not solve the problem. A child who has been a victim of bullying will be at further risk to be picked on, particularly in a new school setting.

Summary

In this chapter I have discussed a variety of situations that six- to twelve-year-old children experience. All make the children and their parents concerned and apprehensive. However, most of them can be dealt with successfully in a short space of time.

Sometimes the real reason for a child behaving in a particular way remains hidden. Take, for example, the child who refuses to go to school. She hides the real message and indeed often may not be aware of why she is avoiding school.

Effective communication with children is not always straightforward. You have to work at it, progressing from cooing to her when she is six months old to discussing her relationships and worries when she is sixteen years of age.

Parents may find the following suggestion helpful when they are trying to develop their family's communication.

1. Watch your mood. Speak simply and clearly and use simple language.

2. Listen. Allow your child to have her say. Do not interrupt.

3. Make time for family discussions. Exchange ideas on current interests with your children. Encourage all the children to make a contribution.

4. Focus on feelings. Ask your son how he is feeling. When he comes in from school and moodily dumps his bag in the hall, instead of shouting at him to put the bag elsewhere, try saying 'I see you're bothered about something'.

5. Paint, draw, exchange stories, watch a film with your children. These activities can give you a great deal of information about your child's world.

6. Divide and conquer. Bring one child with you to a sporting fixture or out for a walk. Having a son or daughter on their own with you gives them an opportunity to talk much more openly and to feel closer to you.

7. Maintain a close relationship with the children's teacher and tell her when you are worried about anything in particular.

The teenage years (1)

Paul Andrews SJ

The teenage years (1)

Much talk about the teenage years tends to focus on the sort of problems that parents have to face during these years. Their job is more often to live with these problems than to find solutions for them. When you were a teenager, did you want your parents to help solve your problems? Books or experts are of little help here. You are the only expert on your children, and you rear them from your own strengths and weaknesses, and from your own experience of life.

It is difficult to stand back from yourself as the parent of a teenager. The issues tend to be too urgent and important to allow for much quiet reflection. You see habits developing, both good and bad, which are going to be there for a long time. Your daughter is facing work in school that will have a direct bearing on her career prospects. Your son starts to grow, becomes louder and is impossible to ignore. Day by day they may create crises that impel you to make decisions. You seem at times to be struggling for survival as a parent, unable to see the wood for the trees, but it may help to look at the *tasks* rather than at the problems of these years:

> Coming to terms with a new body
> Coming to terms with the peer-group
> Learning to deal with the opposite sex
> Achieving greater independence of one's parents
> Choosing and preparing for a career
> Developing one's own values about life — a long, slow business.

A new body

It is pleasant to report that we are rearing bigger, healthier children than we were ourselves. Over the last hundred years, in industrialised countries, the beginning of puberty (marked by the start of menstruation in girls; less easily dated in boys) has come earlier and earlier, in fact by four months every ten years. So, today, the average girl of thirteen is at the same stage of physical development as her mother was at the age of fourteen, thirty years ago.

Children are growing bigger, and developing sexually, at an earlier date. Presumably the trend will level out eventually. The first careful Irish research into the matter found that, on average, Irish girls began menstruating at age thirteen-and-a-half. Girls from higher socio-economic brackets and urban areas tend to mature earlier, while those with poor nutrition, chronic illness, psychological problems or who take excessive exercise begin menstruation later.

The sequence of growth in boys differs from that in girls. In girls, the growth spurt — getting taller by four inches a year instead of the two-and-a-half that has been the average through childhood — precedes the other signs of puberty: the swelling of breasts, the growth of pubic hair, and the first period. In boys the growth spurt usually comes later, after the changes in the genitals, the appearance of pubic and facial hair, and the first emission of semen.

As in so many matters, we know more about other countries than about our own. There are few clear figures for Irish boys. Medical examinations in Dublin primary schools established that our children are growing bigger earlier. The average twelve-year-old boy in 1970 was about an inch taller than in 1960. In Britain the sharp spurt in growth generally comes after the fourteenth birthday, but that is only an average.

Children may enter puberty at any time from nine to seventeen, but those at the extremes, who develop much earlier or much later than the norm, do not feel normal. The late developer feels that he is the odd man out, with a high-pitched voice compared with the deepening sounds of his fellow pupils; and with a child's hairless body that may draw comments in the changing-rooms from his hairier classmates.

I can remember a bright, quiet boy whom I taught, reserved rather than outgoing; as clever as they come, a hard and ambitious worker, and a good swimmer and footballer up to the age of twelve. Mark's growth spurt came late. At about age fourteen, he became so conscious of his smallness that he gave up swimming and football rather than put up with the comments in the changing-room. His handwriting became small and crabby, he grew despondent, and his work gradually deteriorated to the point where teachers were saying that he would have to repeat a year.

Mark was a healthy boy, he was eating well, and his parents were both reasonably tall; there was no physical reason for him to be small. Doctors could do nothing. His parents were understanding and concerned. Nobody was to blame, and it was no use moralising or exhorting Mark; that only made him feel worse. He knew well how badly he was doing on all fronts, but he felt inadequate every time he looked in the mirror, or spoke aloud in class. As with most teenage problems, the solution was to be found not in intervention but in the passing of time.

Mark made it in time. By the beginning of fifth year he had grown by several inches, was shaving and had become deep-voiced, developed a bolder, more confident handwriting, and was able to qualify for medical school after his Leaving Certificate.

There is no denying that early developers have an advantage. Generally they do better both at sports and in social relationships, and are even more successful academically, probably all stemming from the self-confidence that bodily maturing can bring.

Yet the late developers have their own advantages. Their personalities are more formed and their intelligence is more alert by the time they face the excitements and anxieties that accompany sexual maturity. Even their small stature can help. We have seen superb sportsmen who in their teens were small but yet nippy and agile, able to run rings round their lumbering opponents.

Whether children develop early or late, the years of physical change are uncomfortable to live through. Your daughter will lose a sense of the continuity of her body, and will not know how she appears to the world, as her limbs stretch and her face grows spotty. The gangly arms and legs stretch; so many fifteen-year-olds experience a temporary but embarrassing clumsiness when they reach for a glass and their hand hits it sooner than they expect and knocks it over. Most teenagers are sensitive to their changing body, and can be critical of it.

What can parents do? With the late developer, in danger of being rejected by her group as still just a kid, you can encourage hobbies and accomplishments that are respected by her classmates but in which small size is no disadvantage: playing a musical instrument, or taking up certain sports where weight and height matter less.

If you would like to give more precise reassurance to your children, calculate the average of their father's and mother's height. Add 10cm for a son; subtract 10cm for a daughter, and you will have a fair idea of the height each child will be at age nineteen.

Make sure that your children understand that puberty can begin at nine or at seventeen. If your teenager is at one of the extremes, while she may feel out of step with the group, she is not abnormal, and will catch up and reach her natural growth.

Do you and your teenagers realise that sexual development need not go in step with increasing height? Small boys who are hairy and sexually developed should be told that in time they will make up the needed inches. Tall girls with flat, hairless bodies must be reassured that their sexual development will come about without them necessarily getting taller.

Teach your teenagers to like their bodies by liking them yourself. Show your pleasure at being able to swop sweaters with your daughter, your admiration for a son who can shift furniture or suitcases with newly discovered strength.

Treat your children according to their maturity rather than their height. Do not plunge an early developer into premature adulthood, nor prolong the childhood of one who is simply slow to grow.

Relate to the person rather than to the body, but do not forget how large their body looms in the worries of your teenagers. Your daughter may be embarrassed by the size of her breasts, your son by the prominence of his ears. Both of them may endure slagging because of this. The one practical thing parents can do is to understand and make allowances.

Moods

One result of the body's changes is familiar to every parent:

adolescent moodiness, the violent swings from excited highs to depressive lows. One moment your daughter sees nothing worth living for, her whole future is overshadowed by the need to work for the Leaving Certificate. An hour later she has been invited to a party and is on top of the world, turning the house upside down while deciding what to wear. Part of these changes of mood is the result of the hormonal changes that affect her emotional life. Part is because she is no longer sure what she looks like, or how she is seen, at a time when the views of her friends, girls and boys, are important. She is asking herself major questions, seeing life in the long term for the first time, and it is easy for adults to forget what a daunting prospect that is.

How do you react to a teenager's moods? One piece of good advice is that what you show by your actions is more important than what you say. Your daughter needs your stability, your capacity to live with her ups and downs, as a promise that one day she will be able to get back on an even keel.

Depression

If your teenage daughter is sad, she may be reacting to the sort of blows that can upset a fourteen-year-old: being ditched by a friend, failing an exam, shifting to a different class, having to wear a band on her teeth, moving out of a familiar house or neighbourhood, getting a hard time from a teacher, or worst of all, sensing serious tension between her parents. We have all survived such blows, but they make the world feel very bleak.

If your daughter is upset in this way, just at a time when her resistance is low — when she is tired, or physically out of sorts, or suffering from menstrual problems — then the blow will hit her twice as hard, and her recovery will be slower. She will need the support that parents give best — not trying to moralise, or jolly her out of it, but ensuring rest, physical recovery, an easing of pressure, and an ear ready to listen.

Aggression

Apart from depression, you may often have to cope with aggression. This is a mysterious thing, more destructive in humans than in other animals. Unlike the desire for food, sex or sleep, aggression is not satisfied by being indulged. Fighting boys or quarrelling girls do not become peaceful when they are allowed to get at one another. They become even more angry.

We all know the physical signs. When he is angry, a boy has a faster pulse rate, he breathes more rapidly and is less sensitive to fatigue and pain. He is also less open to arguments. When he comes home in a bad temper, although you may be weary yourself and annoyed that he is so grumpy, there is no point in saying so for the moment. First accept him as he is. Show that you know what he feels like — he does not enjoy being grumpy — and then you will have some chance of being heard. You can accept angry feelings; they are innocent, they come unbidden. Our children have to learn the difference between these involuntary feelings, and wilfully acting on them by abusing others in word or deed.

Because anger affects the body, it is usually wise to look for some constructive way that your teenager can use up his physical energy other than by fighting. Football, running, working in the garden, riding a bike — all can help the anger subside. You have not pinned the blame on your son, or received an apology. You have simply diverted the energy that otherwise might have gone into a fight, and you have kept calm, away from the centre of the hurricane.

The first and last remedy is to be serene, to show him the sort of behaviour you want from him. He does not like losing control, and if he sees you doing so, it makes him more panicky. Our children's anger provokes our own, and some fathers even feel it is their duty to be visibly furious and sometimes violent. Whatever about duty, it does not work. Do not let your son's way of treating you determine your way of treating him.

How they look

It is difficult to survive your teenager's years without some battles, but you must choose your battlefield, rather than be exhausted by an endless series of skirmishes. You could spend all your energy and time arguing about clothes and appearance, but why bother? It is obvious not only that styles change and go on changing, but that the makers of clothes, hairstyles and jewellery tend to call the tune, and to keep changing the tune, so that today's buy will be unwearable in a few weeks' time.

On a Friday evening you see young women rushing home and an hour later going back out in clothes so similar to those their friends are wearing that they might well be in uniform. You may resent so much expense going on clothes that soon will be discarded, and if your son or daughter is to learn the value of money, you must work out a way of budgeting for clothes, while allowing your children the space to develop their own taste and style. I know a man in his thirties who still relies on his mother to choose his shirts and ties for him — and she enjoys his dependence! It is little compliment to her that he still cannot choose for himself.

You are more likely to be bothered by the opposite: a boy or girl who tries out everything, even the most far-out clothes, to see 'Is it me?'. Much of teenage behaviour can be described as testing a variety of scripts to see which one will suit your part in life. If that is your son or daughter, take comfort in the fact that they want to 'look good'. You may remember a time when you could not get your son to the bathroom, or to care about how he looked. Now he wants to look good, and a large part of looking good is looking *right*. What looks right in a disco looks wrong when one is visiting relations, or is out on a sunny beach.

At fifteen your daughter wants her clothes to convey the message *I belong here*. If she is persuaded into attending a function against her will, she may want her clothes to proclaim: *I'm only here under pressure. I belong somewhere else.*

Before you confront your daughter about her clothes, prepare yourself this way. First, try to remember remarks made to you as a teenager about your clothes, by parents or others who mattered to you. Remember the compliments: 'Red really looks good on you', 'I love your hair like that'. Remember the negative remarks or silences that often were interpreted as disapproval. Remember how such remarks counted with you, whether to please or infuriate, and then weigh well what you are going to say to your teenager.

Work out what you feel about her clothes, and why — the real reasons are often not on the surface. Try completing the sentence:

I feel ————— (angry/ashamed/delighted, or whatever) when Fiona wears ————— (describe the clothes and the situation) to ————— (church, shopping, etc) because ————— (describe why you feel that way).

Then you have to decide is it worth making a fuss. You may feel that she is giving a bad example to her younger sister, or that she will displease her school principal or a potential employer. On the other hand, a confrontation may well lead to a big family row.

Possibly your daughter thinks your own style of dress is fuddy-duddy or pompous, that she is embarrassed by your appearance at school functions as much as you may be by her on the street. Has she ever said as much? Her style may look far-out to you but be entirely appropriate and right for her — or perhaps a daring experiment she wants, after much agonising, to try out on her friends. Almost certainly she will have changed her style in a year or two, and may then be embarrassed by photographs of what she wears now.

New friends

One of the humbling experiences for the parents of teenagers is to see their advice ignored, while their children will accept the same notion, put much more crudely, from their pals down the road. A teenager is trying to become independent of his parents, to form his own opinions, to find a style that carries his signature. He has not yet got the wisdom or strength to form judgements or values on his own, so initially he lines up with a group of friends with whom he can share his uncertainties and try out a personal style.

We are not talking about one or two friends, but about a 'teenage culture'. In the 1950s, the hucksters of the Western world discovered that a large population of teenage boys and girls were living at home and earning money in part- or full-time jobs, with few commitments and a certain amount of disposable income. A huge market was created and served, with blue denim, T-shirts, constantly changing styles of hair, boots, runners and shirts, with magazines, and above all, with music, first in records, then tapes and compact discs, music in a thousand distinctive styles, but all *young* music. Put together, it amounted to a separate culture, which at its most extreme conveyed values hostile to those of most adults, and shouted *sex, drugs and rock and roll*.

To help their teenage children, parents must first remember their own teens, especially how important their friends were. More or less unrecognised feelings from the past affect how you relate to your teenager today. Part of that relationship could be unacknowledged envy. Do you dress in teenage fashions? Your children will have an opinion on this. Do you sometimes compete with your teenager about who has the more hectic social life? Do you try to join in your teenager's social activities? Do you flirt with his/her friends? Do you get worked up about the amount of money your teenager spends on clothes, hairstyles and make-up?

If the answer to some of these questions is 'Yes', then you are admitting to some envy of your teenager. This is understandable. Their generation has huge opportunities and joys open to them — clothes of shapes, colours and textures that we never knew, the possibility of travel, of sports and skills, and access to information through the computer revolution — that enhance life in a thousand ways.

How do you feel about all this? Afraid of the risks your teenagers are running? Embarrassed at how foolish they look or sound? Ashamed because they seem to reject all you have taught them about how to behave? Envious of the bright new world they are inheriting? Redundant and old when you see them living their own lives at a pace you could not manage, apparently no longer needing you?

Parents can take some comfort from the fact that most teenagers share their parents' basic values. Two-thirds of adolescents see their parents (sometimes one, sometimes both) as the most important people in their lives; they value their opinions and do not want to disappoint them. They often disagree with them on matters of lifestyle, such as clothes, hairdos, make-up, music, the time of coming home at night or of going to bed. But, by their mid-twenties, most have settled down to a view and style of life remarkably like their parents' — not what their parents preach, but what they are.

So while you may worry in these teenage years, the most important message may be the one Bishop Camara gave to his colleagues in Brazil: 'My brothers, watch how you live. Your life may be the only gospel your children will ever read.' Our children, with their sharp wit and searing criticism, force us to reconsider our own life, and whether we live by what we propose for them.

Bishop Camara's advice is true in obvious ways. Parents who smoke have less authority in deterring their children from smoking. Parents who, when stressed, seek comfort from tablets and alcohol, are less able to dissuade their children from taking drugs, especially alcohol.

It is also true in less obvious ways. I knew a girl whose father was fooling around with much younger women in a country town. The daughter began to behave in a conspicuously sluttish way, and this forced her father, who was ranting at her behaviour, to face up to his own.

Undesirable friends

Some issues cause particular pain to parents. Suppose you see your daughter becoming friendly with a girl whom you dislike? Choosing a friend is so important for her that you are obviously reluctant to criticise her choice. It is better for her to make and break relationships herself during these years, when she is trying to learn the art of friendship. Only forbid a friendship if it is absolutely necessary, such as if the chosen friend is anti-social, aggressive, a thief, or a drug-taker. Otherwise, the less critical you can be of her friends, the better. They need each other, and if your daughter knows that you accept this, and are prepared to put up with freakish clothes, loud music, and enormous appetites for coffee and biscuits, you are more likely to stay in touch with what is happening to her during these years. They are your daughter's friends, not yours. No doubt she is less than enthusiastic about some of your friends.

Loners

Let us suppose that your daughter seems to have no friends and you worry about this. Does she? Is she miserable on her own? Introverted children, who are happy with just one or two friends and can play by themselves quite contentedly, are just as normal as the extroverts who like to be the life and soul of the party.

Sometimes a girl who is lonely and miserable can put up a good front in school. When she finds that she is not part of any group, she spends her break with a book or a solitary game, and persuades herself that she is so busy, she does not need friends. In fact she may rebuff other children who try to make friends. You will know whether she is unhappy or not, and whether she is able to join in with others when she wants to. In the early years of secondary school it is particularly painful to be excluded from a group. I doubt if there is anything that causes girls and boys more hurt than that sense of exclusion, often so distressing that they cannot admit to it themselves.

Some children are shy, even at home. What were you like as a teenager? Shyness sometimes is hereditary. It is also affected by the life we have lived. A number of things may mark you as different: being overshadowed by a bright sister or brother, or an acute experience of failure without much support to help you through it, or the insecurity that comes from being moved repeatedly from school to school, having to get used to different customs and styles, and feeling an outsider, nervous that your voice, your accent, your clothes make you different.

One thing you obviously should *not* do, and that is talk about your child's shyness. She must not be teased or scolded for it. It is stupid to tell her not to be shy; she cannot help it, and ridicule can do nothing but harm. If you focus on a pothole when you are driving, you are likely to hit it. If you focus on fear and shyness, you will find it hard to escape from them. The remedy must be indirect: build up your daughter's confidence by enhancing her skills and encouraging interests that will bring her in touch with others.

Do you make it easy for her to have friends in to the house? Can she introduce them to you without fearing a critical or unwelcoming eye? Within the home, she may find it hard to make her voice heard at a chatty table, so it is doubly important for you to ensure that she gets an appreciative hearing when she does say something, and make her feel that she has something worthwhile to say. Remember that she is probably easily embarrassed about clothes and appearance, so let her wear what will not make her look odd or conspicuous outside the home.

Coming home late

During the teenage years, many of the issues that make for rows are really about your teenagers' conflict of loyalty between their family and friends. If your son is due home at eleven and comes home an hour late, it is more likely to be from reluctance to break away from the group, than from a desire to disobey you. If parents read it as disobedience, the conflict is sharpened, not understood or resolved.

As your teenagers get older, they probably will be allowed out more often at night, and be permitted to come home later. Conditions vary so much between families that I believe only two norms are possible: that parents should always know where their children are; and that if children cannot be home at the arranged time, they should phone to let their parents know.

Helping or hindering?

If you see your teenager's friends as a good part of her growing up, how do you see yourself? Are you helping or hindering that process? Look at the list given here of common ways in which teenagers spend time with their friends, and then consider the ways in which you might help or hinder them.

Teenage occupation	Help	Hinder
Sit chatting in the bedroom.	Leave them to it.	Insist that they sit with the family.
Going to a disco.	Give them a lift home.	Say it's too late to be out or even go with them!
Staying overnight at a friend's house.	Trust them to behave.	Keep phoning.
Trips out with friends.	Be encouraging, provided you know the friends.	Point out all the things that could go wrong.
Holidays away from home with friends.	Say OK if it is an organised holiday.	Keep harping on about not getting into trouble.
Hanging around on street corners.	Ideally, give them a cosy room to use themselves.	Do not allow it.
Teenage parties in your house.	Stay in the house.	Try to be in the same room.
Conversations about heroes.	Listen.	Mock them.

However wise and calm you may be at a distance, it is still painful to lose your daughter — who has been such a companion to you — to her friends who seem to matter more to her now. It is painful when she seeks advice from or spends more time with her friend's parents, or with an adult friend, than with you. It hurts when you become aware of secrets in her life to which you are not privy. There is no sense in trying to go back to the relationship you had during her childhood. Her new confidants and friends are a sign of her growth, and the new relationship you have with her will be based on your acceptance of her as a separate but loved daughter, with her own personality and style, which in all likelihood will emerge, after these confused years, as similar to your own.

Drugs and peer pressure

We know something about the effect of drugs, and about their use among old and young addicts. Among teenagers, two drugs stand out as much more dangerous than the rest — alcohol and nicotine. Two-thirds of our teenagers have used each of these at some time, compared with about 13 per cent who have used cannabis, 13 per cent who have sniffed solvents (responsible for about ten Irish deaths in 1988); 6 per cent who have abused tablets of various sorts, and 1-2 per cent who have used cocaine or heroin, which were responsible for twenty to thirty deaths in 1988.

The propaganda and changed attitude about smoking have had some effect on the young, and have saved them from a habit that would claim a heavy portion of their earnings or pocket-money, and give them, with time, less pleasure and more likelihood of serious illness.

Public propaganda about alcohol is mostly for rather than against, and focuses successfully on the young and attractive. Peer pressure to drink is enormous. Nearly a quarter of Irish teenagers have been drunk six or more times (the proportion is higher in older teenagers). By any standards these youngsters are well on the way to abusing alcohol and being at risk of addiction. Like nicotine, alcohol kills, usually by accident, and it corrupts the quality of life in many families.

Young people who declared their intention of not taking alcohol as teenagers are less likely to become addicts. There is a lot to be said for the firm purpose embodied in the Confirmation pledge. Even apart from its spiritual value, it greatly increases the prospect of the youngster being in control of the drink habit.

There are parts of the country where cannabis is easily available, and it is pressed on the young as non-addictive. Unlike alcohol and nicotine, cannabis does not kill, but it interferes with study, affects short-term memory, turns the bright student into an average one, and the average one into a dull one. Traces linger in the fatty tissue for up to three weeks after a 'joint', and recently some sinister links have been discovered between cannabis and cancer.

It is easy to preach about the danger of drugs, but what about guidelines? Your first job as a parent is to *understand why* your child is puffing, sniffing or drinking. Most teenagers take drugs because they want to experiment and see how far they can go with taking risks. It is a way of asserting control over their own body which, in childhood, was mother's to worry about.

Most teenagers will learn to set their own limit. The drug may fulfil a temporary need. It may give relief from anxiety. It may calm an angry mood. It may make the youngster feel acceptable to her friends. It may remove her shyness. It may just be fun.

As your daughter grows into a greater self-confidence, she will find the drug an unsatisfactory solution because it reduces her individuality. Teenagers can find human, non-chemical ways to deal with their anger and to calm their nervousness.

A few teenagers use drugs as a solution to depression or to severe disturbance, and you will see yourself whether this is the case with your son or daughter.

An educational group in Dublin has suggested five guidelines under the letters that make up the word 'teach'.

T is for *Talking*, which includes knowing something about drugs, listening to your children, keeping communication open through all the disagreements of the teenage years, being honest about your own beliefs and values, and not letting disagreement be seen as rejection.

E is for *Example*. Children who see their parents coping with shock, stress or bad moods without crying 'I need a drink', or reaching for other chemical help, are themselves more likely to manage stress without palliatives.

A is for *Alternative activities*. So many teenagers go to the pub because there are few other options. As soon as our children move abroad to less pub-centred cultures, they discover more active and fulfilling ways of spending their spare time. Being busy with a variety of leisure pursuits is a positive way of preventing addiction.

C is for *Confidence*. How many boys and girls tank up in order to gain Dutch courage to ask a partner to dance or come out on a date. Genuine confidence will grow over the years because of the attitudes of parents who do not put their children down, but take every occasion to support them and show affection, and forgive, or seek forgiveness, after a row.

H is for *How*: how to say 'no' to drugs; how to walk silently away from a stranger who solicits; how to continue to say 'no' to a persistent friend, without being more offensive than is necessary.

What do you ask of your teenager? To keep you in touch with the realities of their life, so that you know if they drink, and why. If it is because the pub is the only place to meet friends, then perhaps you can make the home more available. You may have advice to offer on how to refuse a drink, or a lift home from a drinker; or to share the price of a taxi if that is the only way they can get home. Heavy teenage drinkers tend to come either from resolutely anti-drink families, or from families where there is heavy drinking. Parents who treat drinking as ordinary, moderate behaviour are more likely to have children who do the same. Your aim in this is not just your own peace of mind, but for your teenagers to learn to manage their own life and health sensibly.

The other sex

Girls must learn to get on with boys, and boys with girls. Parents have the right to pass on what they want to pass on, and no two will be quite the same. What do you want for your teenage children? That they would achieve a certain inner freedom about sexual matters, be neither prudish nor promiscuous. That they would achieve sufficient control not to be repeatedly led by their sexual appetites into making fools of themselves. That their sexuality would become a way of relating lovingly to another person, not a means of exploitation or self-indulgence.

What can parents do to further these objectives? They must start early, or they may be unable to start at all. It is not just what parents say that counts. They pass on a sense of their own bodies, of their sexuality, as a good and central part of themselves. They pass on their ease in touching and embracing one another. With that, they make themselves open to questions. They accept that there is no such thing as an improper question from their children; that father is as open to questioning as mother. If a child has the curiosity to ask a question, then parents have a duty to answer it.

The opportunities for sex education come especially from shared experiences in the family, such as watching television together. This is a far better vehicle for education than the classic situation where father summons son for an awkward chat on the facts of life. If the father is embarrassed, then the talk will be ineffectual, because children will want to end the interview as quickly as possible.

The ideal starting point for sex education is the phantasies and curiosities of children. If young children are asked not to speak about but to repress them, then it will be difficult to find an alternative starting point. If their questions and comments are responded to, then there is some hope that, in their early teens, they may share their worries and questions with their parents.

There is no aspect of teenage life where peer pressure is as relentless as in sexual questions. Look at the questions thrown up by twelve- and thirteen-year-olds in the open sessions organised by schools: 'I go to the park 'cos I wouldn't have friends if I didn't. But fellas do awful rude things to us there. Yet I want friends.' 'Girls call us wimps if we don't frenchie them. I'd be afraid to.' Girls in sixth class say that you have to pretend to be interested in boys or you will be left out of the chat and laughs. Group standards are sometimes set by one or two untypical leaders. Many boys and girls are nervous about talk of sex and unready for the sort of knowing references, often borrowed from TV and bandied in half-understood ways by children who are hardly into puberty.

So there is a great need for parents to be open to any question, and to answer it honestly and calmly, without shock or an implied moral judgement on their children. It is too late to start that openness when puberty looms. It must begin early. This does not mean having set answers and prepared speeches, but rather a readiness to listen to worries about dating, oral sex, homosexuality, masturbation, the use of contraceptives and countless other questions that torment teenagers, caught between intense peer-pressure and gossip on the one hand, and an unformed or nervous conscience on the other.

If you yourself feel confused or uncertain about some of these questions, perhaps because you received no help from your own parents, admit it; you do not have to pretend to know everything. We have to teach our children to be able to make moral judgements for themselves, and that they do not have to play sex games just because their friends do (or say they do).

If you feel that your children will not talk or listen to you, what help can be given them? A good deal is done by those schools that organise, either at the end of primary or the beginning of secondary, formal sex education sessions for pupils and their parents, so that parents know clearly what is happening. Obviously much of what is presented there will be known to the children, but they will be able to correct their half-knowledge, and to ask questions about things that bother them.

Homosexuality

In many families it is hard enough to talk about sex, but much harder to face the fact that a son or daughter may be homosexual. Not that homosexuality is a taboo subject. Sexual behaviour and its variations are the staple diet of the soap operas; but that is at a remove from life. The fact that the airwaves are preoccupied with sex has not made it any easier for young people, especially boys, to gain confidence in their own sexuality as it blossoms in their teenage years. On the contrary: the more boys banter one another with the sexual slagging and double-meaning jokes of the comedies and TV soaps, the more confused they may become about their rate of development. It is no longer a case of your fifteen-year-old son feeling his body grow, listening to his inner desires, and discovering how attractive the other sex has become both in phantasy and in real life. That natural growth has been tarnished by the media style that turns girls into sex-objects (most jokes are made from the man's viewpoint) and sex into a matter of flippancy. Any group of mid-teen boys in a slagging mood will consider that a teacher or boy is gay because of his voice, or gestures, or even because of his shoes or the pattern of his shirt.

A number of boys are on the edge of a swimming pool. One dives in, shouting 'Last one in is a queer', and he has forgotten the remark before he surfaces. But the phrase may stay quivering in the soul of the last one in, who is just at that stage of wondering about his own sexual leanings.

Other memories may feed your son's anxiety. He is very close to his mother — but then so are many macho boys. He once enjoyed dressing up in his sister's clothes at Hallowe'en — but so did other high-spirited boys. He is deeply attached to his best friend Paul — but best friends are a terribly important anchor in the early teens when the other sex still seems threatening.

At age fifteen, even physical or sexual intimacy with another boy need not be significant as regards long-term sexual orientation. It can be alarming for you as a parent when such an incident comes to your notice, but do not panic because of fear that it will turn your son into a homosexual. In this, as in the still more troubling case of molestation by an adult, the situation is helped if the parent remains unruffled.

However, these and other factors, capped by the slagging of his classmates, can cause something approaching panic in a boy who is trying to find his own inner balance and is expected to make and state an outward sexual choice. The panic can be worse in a single-sex boarding school, where an older boy may find his phantasy centring on a younger boy, and feel himself doomed to homosexuality.

'Doomed' is a strong word, but it expresses what is commonly felt by boys in this state of homosexual panic: the fear of orientation towards a state of life that can carry a terrible burden of insult and loneliness and the sense of being an outsider. Probably only a tiny minority of those who experience homosexual panic go on to a homosexual way of life. There are two dangers. One is that the boy or girl may fail to recognise the panic for what it is, a passing phase, and think of themselves, unjustifiably, as gay. The other is that they be seduced into homosexual practices, which could confirm them in their fears and orientation.

Parents can help, in an indirect way:

First, avoid sexual labelling. Do not treat tenderness, caring, artistic interests or a flair for clothes as signs of homosexuality in a boy. He will become a man in his own way, and the ways of manhood are far broader than the macho style touted by some overgrown schoolboys.

Second, avoid sexual teasing. Many adolescent boys give their best energies to sport or academic activities, and are not helped by remarks about their lack of girlfriends. If you tease your son as though he is peculiar, you risk making him think that he is.

Thirdly, remember that, while we do not know exactly why some adults are homosexual, we do know that their preference cannot be changed at will nor prevented by exhortation in adolescence. So help your son with his anxiety when it surfaces, and stay close or at least accessible to him throughout his development.

Independence

All our effort as parents is to make our children able to find their own way in the world, to become independent of us. Most of us want to enable our child not just to survive, but to be a good person. Goodness means more than keeping the law; moral goodness goes beyond what the law covers, and sometimes the law sanctions things that are morally evil. Goodness involves having values, a sense of right and wrong, and respect for other people's needs. From watching children grow through different sorts of childhood, we know a good deal about the sort of rearing that creates inner values, such that young people learn to make up their own minds.

First, the bond with parents is one based on *affection rather than power*. True, young children are in the power of their parents — and of teachers and other authorities — but the values they will adopt come from those who love them and whom they love. As the teenage years pass, parents run out of power but not of affection. Sometimes, in the middle of a row over staying out late or drinking, you may wish that you could crack the whip more effectively. That might produce a short-term obedience to your orders, but only the love that binds you to your children will help them to make your values their own.

Secondly, there is some *consistency* in the way parents rear their children. Father's stance is consistent with mother's, though perhaps not identical in emphasis; and both parents make roughly the same demands on children from day to day and year to year.

Thirdly, if you want your children to adopt your values, you must make moral demands on them, challenge them to be just, self-controlled, courageous and forgiving; not just because it makes for a more comfortable life at home, but because it is good for their development.

Fourthly, as far as possible, the *sanctions on children's misbehaviour should be personal rather than physical*. You can correct them without hitting them; it happens all over the world, and it works. If parents were reared with a good deal of slapping, they sometimes feel that they are not serious unless they hit out. Again, this can produce short-term results, but inner values depend on a trust in your own moral authority, and the power of your disapproval. Violence towards teenagers can lead to a rough house and estrangement. Often parents have to be ready to state their disapproval, follow it up by withholding favours or by grounding the boy or girl. Force will be counter-productive.

Fifthly, when the chance arises, *explain, reason and negotiate* your position, rather than impose it dogmatically. When you have to correct, do it in private, rather than in front of others; shaming your teenage son or daughter often leads not to repentance but to resentment.

Follow your conscience

If this all seems too soft and permissive, let me add a word about conscience. There will be times when teenage children will protest that they must make their own decisions, do their own thing, and sometimes parents, afraid of losing their children's love, imply *Do your own thing and I will support you*. That is a different and distorted message from *Follow your conscience*.

Many of us lived through authoritarian teaching, by parents and teachers, which allowed us no room for questioning. Yet the old catechism told us to obey our lawful superiors 'in all that is not sin'. This implies that everyone should judge whether he/she is being told to do something evil in the name of authority. Everyone has to account first to her or his conscience.

If this is true for adults, it is also true for bright and educated teenagers. They are no longer parroting their teachers' moral judgements, but are forming value judgements that carry personal conviction.

Does this mean that *sincerity* matters most? *I am doing this because I feel it is right for me.* No, we are not talking about feelings but about judgements, which means that you have to use your head. You are not looking for *your* truth but for *the* truth. It is objectivity that is being sought, not sincerity. The Watergate conspirators or the My Lai murderers would probably have claimed that they *sincerely* felt that they should obey orders when they carried out their criminal acts. They did not ask about the injustice and violence being done to others.

Suppose your twenty-year-old daughter tells you that she feels she should move in with her boyfriend for an indefinite period. Immediately you think of the prospect of her having a baby, who either is not wanted or who does not have a stable parental couple to rear it. What worries you as parents is your moral position and duty.

The father is tempted to use his authority either to threaten his daughter or to throw her out of the house. That is not a moral reaction but a physical one. It is found often in well-intentioned people who are keenly aware of youth's limitations and who wish to protect them from doing harm to themselves or others.

Another part of you fears a confrontation with your daughter. You can be so afraid of appearing uptight and straight-laced that you tiptoe around potential disagreements. You fear that if you contradict her you will lose her. You are also painfully aware that you have warned her against some things that she now considers either harmless or even desirable, and you do not want to make her unnecessarily guilty. And so you are tempted to go along with what she wants, to avoid a row or rupture.

What position is there between coercion (which seldom works), and *laissez-faire*, which is abandoning any moral stance? You can trust your moral authority, even if you cannot or will not back it with force. *As your parent, I will never reject you; I am always on your side. But I believe that what you plan to do is potentially destructive and wrong. If you do it, you may hurt yourself and others. I do not question your sincerity, and do not want you to stop thinking for yourself, but I have a responsibility to myself and to you to stand up for what I believe, and to caution you against behaviour that I consider irresponsible.*

This is a position that springs from love and can be maintained with love, even if your daughter walks out on you. She will walk out knowing that she can count on you. Perhaps she will stay. Sometimes a young person, even as old as twenty, unconsciously wants, more than anything else, to have some adult say No.

Summary

For a hard-headed but sympathetic summary, I can think of nothing better than a letter that an Australian headmaster used to write to the parents of his boys as they turned fifteen:

My purpose in writing is to prepare you for an imminent change in the relationship between yourself and your son. The affectionate small boy who has been your pride and joy is about to undergo such a transition that you may well begin to wonder whether you have produced a monster. Perhaps you have already begun to wonder where you have gone wrong, or what you have done to deserve his new-found anger.

Do not despair — ride out the storm, be firm and affectionate. At this moment when he seems to need you least, he in fact needs you most. Take a stand about the principles you regard as fundamental. Give him rope about the less important things; do not worry too much about what he wears or the length of his hair. Comfort yourself with the knowledge that his present moods are transitory.

If you do this and stand firm as a rock in the midst of his tempestuous life, the small boy whom you thought you had lost will return to you as a charming young man, well-groomed in appearance and with delightful manners. He will have been well worth waiting for. In the meantime you and I, both of us, are in for one hell of a time!

The teenage years (2)

Frances Fitzgerald

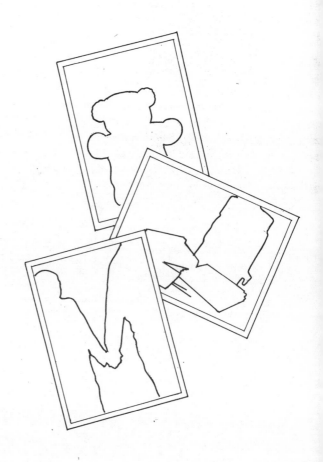

The teenage years (2)

A great deal has been made of 'the generation gap' which supposedly appears as young people reach adolescence. In fact the gap is not nearly as common or wide as we might think. In most families there are disagreements — our children want their hair longer (or shorter!) than we would like, want to wear clothes that to us are strange or unattractive — but generally they will continue to be influenced by us throughout their adolescence. Since it is a period of great change for them, it is important for us to talk to them and support them. The challenge for us as parents is to find ways of responding to our teenagers as they work through the transition to adulthood. Our relationship with our children changes as their more adult personality begins to emerge. The experience of a young person finding his or her way in the wider world is not unlike that of the child starting school, who is beginning the process of separating from the parent. Just as we helped our children take that step, we can help them to deal with the major physical and psychological changes that occur during adolescence.

As they get older, we have to give our children 'more rope' — as a recognition of their growing maturity. From around the age of eleven, our children are moving into adolescence. The physical changes and new feelings may make them moody or withdrawn. They begin to be critical of their parents, but are themselves sensitive to criticism. It is important that parents still communicate well with them, while allowing them space to work out things for themselves.

In the early stages of adolescence children will tend to be busy, talkative and curious, eager to understand the world.

Their parents' views of the world will tend to be accepted unquestionably. By about age twelve this is beginning to change. What Kate at school or Paul down the road has to say about things has as much value as the view of a parent. The twelve-year-old will also be more conscious of the opposite sex.

Thirteen-year-olds tend to be rather reserved. If they spend a lot of time alone, respect their privacy and try not to intrude. Curiously, by age fourteen, young people tend to be more friendly and outgoing, and better able to accept different points of view. Girls may have started their periods, although boys usually are not as physically mature. Endless telephone conversations are quite common at this age as teenagers get to know each other and explore their ideas of themselves, their friends and the world outside. The telephone is used as a safe way of negotiating their place in the world. Parents must see the positive aspects of telephoning, recognising that this is one of the ways that adolescents work out their identity. While trying not to nag them for talking too much on the telephone, we should make our teenagers respect the fact that other family members might like to use the phone too, and that it is costly.

The mid-teenage years are often the most difficult and turbulent. This is a time of maximum experimentation and moodiness as their desire for adult rights is exercised. Parents become anxious that their children might get into trouble, and worried that their values seem so different from their own. At this time, parents must keep a cool head, knowing that the phase will pass. The last thing adolescents need is for their parents to be flying off the handle, overreacting to everything.

By their late teens our children often think of us as 'has beens', old fogeys who are out of touch with the modern world. As their adult personalities and characters develop, we should feel some satisfaction at their growing independence and self-assurance. Yet although eighteen- and nineteen-year-olds may be leaving home and building their own lifestyles, they will still have a great need for the stability of the family. This secure base in their lives helps them to explore the world.

Being a parent

Most of us learn how to be a parent by a mixture of trial and error and the advice of family or friends. Throughout our children's lives the task of being a parent keeps changing as the level of dependency decreases and our relationship with our children develops. Parents carry important hopes and fears for each child. We want them to be happy, to have opportunities to excel, to have satisfying relationships and jobs, to achieve the things they want. However, we must be careful not to use our children to fulfil our own ambitions.

During our children's adolescence, we are helping them to become adults. It can be a rewarding time if we provide support, guidance and advice, while leaving space for our children to do things in their own way.

We are helping our children to separate from us, to create their own identity. Gradually they will build their own lives. It is very important for parents to enjoy their adolescents' growing maturity, success and independence. When they realise that their parents are taking pleasure in their success, our teenagers' confidence will grow even more.

Irish parents often find it difficult to fully enjoy their adolescents' achievements because they do not want to risk spoiling them, but young people need to know that we appreciate their efforts and their achievements.

It is not easy for any parent to let go, to recognise that this growing teenager who a few short years ago was a little child, will soon be an adult. It is especially hard to allow them the space to experiment, to develop a sense of responsibility, if what they want to do does not match our values or our hopes.

Parents must have a great deal of patience and a keen eye to their teenager's talents. We have to put up with the music of the latest groups, a purple bathroom as the attempts to dye everything black goes a little wrong, arguments about staying out, pocket money, clothes, hairstyles, buying a motorbike, studying, and on and on. The major task of adolescence — the development of a separate identity — is achieved through experiments and fads.

It is not easy to see that these things have a place in the young people's development; nor is it easy to believe that their parents will be influential throughout their teenage years. In fact, despite the arguments, the broken rules, the noisiness and the cheeky answers, parents and other adult family members provide an important guide to teenagers as to how adults treat one another. In a family where there are frequent rows, young people will get the idea that this is how relationships should work.

How we face all sorts of issues — relationships, alcohol, our work, sex — inform our young people about a view of the world. We can pass on to our children our hopes for the future, but we can also pass on our anxieties, fears and hang-ups.

The type of relationship we have with our children changes when they reach adolescence. As they begin to explore life more and more without us, they can bring new vitality into a family — new friends and new ideas. If we can keep in mind that the family is a changing unit, then we shall enjoy the next stage of our family's life cycle.

Adolescents hate being talked down to and usually will not respond well to threats. They are coping with the twin pulls: to go back into the safety of the family and childlike behaviour, and to turn away from their family (which they identify with childhood and restrictions) and fly to the beckoning adult world.

Yet adolescents need protection, the firm base of the family from which they can explore the adult world safely. In recent years we have come to realise that adolescents are at risk of being sexually abused. We can protect them against this by knowing where they are and being alert to their distress or anxiety.

Young people need our love, praise and respect as well as reasonable limits. Most of all, they need warm and accepting parents who will support them. Far too few families realise the need for good communication between the different generations. Perhaps we assume that we know how people are, what they are doing and what they want. Sometimes we assume that if people want to talk, they will, but parents should ask direct questions: 'Where are you going?' 'Who are you going out with?' 'What were you doing?' 'Are you drinking?' Parents are surprised when they get more honest and detailed answers than they expect. Do not be afraid to ask; there is no point in putting your head in the sand because you do not want to know.

Young people are most likely to be open about their lives, to confide in us and to seek our help if they are used to seeing us doing that too. If teenagers are used to discussing ideas and venturing opinions at family mealtimes, if plans are made and problems are sorted out with their parents, then they will feel able to raise their own worries. This is not to say that you will agree with or approve of everything they want, but your teenager will not expect that.

Families

In recent years we have begun to realise how much the concept of the family has changed since we were young. Now there are families with two parents, one parent, second families with step-parents, both parents employed, both unemployed, and so on. As families become smaller, the time we have with our children and the length of time we have children at home changes. The role of women in the family is changing also. More women are working outside the home and see child-rearing as a phase of their life rather than their whole life.

We still expect marriage to last a lifetime, even though our lifespan is longer. Yet, although we still want life-long marriages, we accept that many will not last. Many families have one parent or are a combination of two previous families. A greater life expectancy also means a longer retirement.

Families constantly change. The roles and priorities of parents and children evolve as we grow older. Children become adults, parents become grandparents. Sometimes we can lose sight of this, forget that the stresses and strains of being a parent of teenagers will be gone in a few years. The time we spend with them now will be given over to other things as they get older.

Who is in charge?

As children move into the teenage years, they begin to challenge their parents, pushing against the barriers, the rules that limit what they can do and their ability to take decisions for themselves. Backchat and a greater tendency to flare up will be replaced by sarcasm and swearing. Teenagers will try to break or bend the rules, will try to establish new limits to give them more control over their own lives. A parent who has spent many years protecting a child will find the change to a more negotiating relationship difficult to handle. Our task is to help our children to develop respect for other people. An important part of this is to learn to respect their ideas and achievements so that when they test the rules, they know they will be listened to and taken seriously.

Sometimes when adolescents do step out of line, they should be ignored. Learn to separate trivial matters from serious issues, such as coming home drunk, staying out very late. Serious rule-breaking must be dealt with quickly and comprehensively. Before reacting, make sure that you know exactly what has happened.

When dealing with problems, keep a few things in mind:

- Be consistent.

- Set rules that have been thoroughly talked through with your child. Spur of the moment limits usually do not work.

- Offer choices; self-selected rules are more likely to be observed.

- Be clear about what will happen if the rule is broken, and then stick to your guns.

- Do not make idle threats.

Young people often want instant remedies, to experience new things without delay. To have discovered the late disco or an all-night party and not to be allowed go can be devastating to a fifteen-year-old who feels grown up. Waiting until next year may seem perfectly reasonable to us, but to the teenager it is unfair and, anyway, a year seems like forever. Understanding how your teenager feels will help you to talk with them and to establish limits.

One way of building up this relationship is to involve them in family plans and decisions. This means *really* listening to your teenager's viewpoint, and not just handing down pronouncements from the parental throne. Discussing and planning things like family holidays or Christmas arrangements can help to develop a framework for making other decisions. Then, when a decision is being made about something he or she wants to do, the format will be familiar.

If parents can achieve such a relationship, their teenagers will be less likely to break rules or to become disillusioned and angry. As well as the day-to-day issues, parents also have to be able to discuss alcohol, AIDS, drugs and sexual promiscuity calmly and openly.

Sex

Many parents find if difficult to raise or discuss sex with their children. We hope that they will have close relationships with the opposite sex, but we fear the consequences of early sexual activity. Sex marks an important transition to adulthood and we want our children to make that transition when they are emotionally and physically mature.

If we are comfortable with our sexuality, if we enjoy sex as part of a warm, loving and respectful relationship, then we shall be better able to talk openly about sex with our teenage children. We must be able to express our fears about their sexual behaviour *not* as fears about sex itself but about the unhappiness that sex at the wrong time or with the wrong person can bring.

As adolescents develop more intimate relationships, they also will be dealing with 'peer pressure'. Many young people feel that they must have sex because that is what they are told their friends do. If you have helped them to see sex and sexuality as an integral part of loving relationships, then they will be more confident in resisting the pressure to have early and purely physical sex.

Getting it right

The demands on parents can be stressful; few of us have any training for the job and yet we feel that we should always do the right thing. There is no single right way of rearing children, but help can be available. As well as the professional assistance of doctors, teachers and counsellors, we all know people who have already raised a family.

Our children's friends have parents, and speaking with them can be invaluable in setting standards. In a crisis, it can be very helpful to be able to contact other parents for advice. A number of parents agreeing on a particular strategy can give you the confidence to tackle most problems.

Expert advice can be valuable, but it is worth remembering that commonsense and our own instinctive reactions are good guides in most situations. Women often lose their self-confidence and allow themselves to be persuaded by their partner that everything is all right when, deep down, they know that that is not the case.

Making rules

Despite their best efforts to convince you that they do not need rules, most adolescents must be told what the limits are. Your child will respect reasonable limits, but what is reasonable? The rules that we recognised as reasonable when we were teenagers simply may not apply now, so how do you decide?

Finding out what the parents of other young people are doing is a good starting point. Teenagers base their sense of what is reasonable on their understanding of what their friends are allowed to do. Since their 'understanding' may not be entirely accurate, your contact with other parents is important.

Sometimes it is tempting to take a rigid stand, laying down strict rules and insisting that they are to be kept. This approach usually will not work and will lead to big battles. Parents have to learn to give and take. It is very important that they try to understand how a teenager sees things, how easy it is for them to feel misunderstood. Rows about clothes or time-keeping can end up involving the whole family. The more inflexible the rule is, the more difficult it is to resolve the problem. Parenting is a little like industrial relations — two sides trying to find a mutually acceptable solution.

It is worth asking ourselves whether our approach to child-rearing reflects the way we ourselves were reared. If we were not very happy as children, or if we rebelled against our parents, it is likely that we will set up a similar pattern with our own children. How we behave as parents is also tied up with our fears for our children. The balance between our desire to protect them and our need for them to become independent and resilient can be difficult to maintain. Adolescents have to take some risks, to find out for themselves. They must have the space to make mistakes about the unimportant things, so that they can develop the judgement to deal with the important matters.

Alcohol

We drink too much alcohol in Ireland and the large number of young people who drink reflects that fact. The consequences of alcohol abuse include physical and mental illness, family breakdown, violence, road deaths and injuries. Young people need to know about these dangers and to see by our own approach to drinking that we take the risks seriously. If we drink and drive, get drunk or are overly fond of drink, these are strong messages to our children about the importance of alcohol to us in our own lives and our disregard for the implications.

Talk to your children about alcohol, especially when they reach adolescence. If you drink alcohol, apply the sensible warnings to yourself: never drink and drive for example. Let your children see that you are in control when you drink.

Encourage them not to drink alcohol, or to postpone doing so until they are as old as possible. Research shows that the later we begin to take alcohol, the lower the risk of alcoholism and other health problems.

Some parents allow their children to taste drinks as they get older, introducing them to alcohol within the home in order to discourage them from drinking secretly. Other parents opt to wait until their children reach a certain age before allowing them to drink alcohol in the home. Ideally young people will not drink alcohol, but this is an issue that calls for negotiation. Two important points to keep in mind are:

● Treat alcohol the way you want your children to treat it.

● Encourage your children to start drinking as late as possible.

Drugs

Parents must educate their children about non-prescriptive drugs at an early stage. Drugs are readily available, especially within cities and large towns, and young people may be very tempted to take them. Teenagers who are happy and secure, leading busy lives through school, sports and hobbies, are less likely to take drugs.

Parents can show a healthy respect for drugs by only taking prescription medicines and by not taking sleeping pills and antibiotics in a haphazard or self-prescribed way. We sometimes forget that 'drugs' does not just mean heroin and cocaine; pain killers and sleeping tablets can be the first steps to serious drug addiction. How we manage these substances in our homes can give teenagers a healthy respect for their use.

If you suspect or find out that your children are taking drugs, try to discover what type and amount of drug they are taking and where they get them. Seek advice from the school principal or teacher, and from other parents. Most school principals have dealt with the problem at some stage, and early advice is very important. The consequences of drug taking are too serious to hope that the problem will go away.

Breaking the law

Almost everyone breaks the law at some time when they are young. Parents occasionally display double standards. If we are constantly warning our children not to break the law but are breaking the law ourselves — parking in no-parking areas, not paying income tax, driving when we have had too much to drink — then we can hardly expect children to take our warnings seriously.

Our fears are that our children will get in with the 'wrong' crowd and begin to steal or get involved in petty crime. Parents who encourage their children to bring their friends home and who make sure that they know who they are with and where they are going can usually spot when something may be wrong. Being consistent, setting reasonable limits, taking an active interest in their school work and leisure activities, and behaving as though we ourselves respect the law, will all influence how our children behave.

If your child does get into trouble, you must find out what has caused the problem. Feeling let down, angry, depressed and even ashamed are all natural reactions, but we must find ways of resolving the situation. Often the incident may be a symptom of some other problem. Listening to your child's explanation may be extremely difficult when you feel upset and angry, so in some cases it may be worth seeking professional assistance or talking to a parent who has been through a similar experience.

School

A major aspect of any child's adolescence is secondary school. The change from primary to secondary school usually takes place about the same time as the onset of adolescence, reinforcing the new stage in your child's life.

The school your child moves to may well have been selected a long time before. Many parents want to choose the best possible school for their child and will put down his or her name a long time before to secure a place. There may not be a great deal of choice in your neighbourhood, but you should consider a number of things about the kind of school that is best for your child.

Studies have shown that effective schools are those with an emphasis on academic progress, a prompt start to lessons, and a good relationship between teachers and pupils. Such schools are known for recognising their students' achievements.

Talking to other parents, as well as to the teachers, will help you decide whether you like the ethos or attitudes of a particular school and whether it will suit your child.

No two children are alike; their talents and abilities vary greatly. The more you know your child, how they enjoyed primary school and what they like to do, the more likely you are to select a school that will encourage and challenge them. A studious child will do well in a school that emphasises that aspect of development. A child with less of an academic bent may thrive in an environment offering a mixture of academic and non-academic subjects.

Parents must consider the different needs of boys and girls when they are choosing schools. There is evidence that girls perform better academically at single-sex schools. Some boys do not like the emphasis on sport in certain boys' schools. When making your choice, check that subjects are available to both sexes up to the same level. For instance, not all schools offer maths and science at higher levels to girls. Some schools may not be able to offer a mix of practical and academic subjects — having to choose either a language or a technical subject may limit the long-term opportunities of the teenager who is interested in both.

Most schools nowadays offer a range of subjects outside the main subjects required for state exams. Music, sport, clubs and societies provide young people with opportunities to try out new things and to develop different skills, and you should encourage your child to take up some of these activities.

The right school and lots of encouragement and interest in your child's activities can make the six or so years at secondary school an enjoyable experience. An adolescent who is sent to a school where she or he cannot keep up in class will become distressed. Similarly, if they are finding it too easy or not challenging enough, frustration can set in.

Students at secondary school have to plan their homework and their leisure activities. If teenagers can get a good start at secondary school, eventually they will be able to cope with the pressure of state exams. You may have an established routine for homework and for talking with your children about school. If so, keep it going. If not, help your child to work out a routine. Young people should not spend hours on homework, but neither should they seem to be skipping it. If you are interested — and that means asking them what they are doing, as well as telling them to get on with it — they will be more likely to develop a routine.

Education is important and we all want the best for our children, yet it is vital that we do not fall into the trap of pushing them to do things that we like or would like to have done in the past. Wanting your child to have a full education is one thing; wanting them to achieve your life's ambition is something else entirely.

Education should provide young people with the opportunity to develop and explore their talents and interests, to work towards the kind of job or career that interests them. Encouraging your child to achieve what he or she is capable of is a satisfying part of being a parent, but do not push them to attain unrealistic standards.

Parents who take an interest in the school and in how their children are progressing, and who spend time with them on school and other activities, will develop a picture of what is possible and of what makes their son or daughter happy.

Exams

At various times adolescents will have to do exams, usually as a regular part of the school curriculum. The stress level begins to rise when the time for state examinations approaches, especially the Leaving Certificate. Some children sail through exams either because they are particularly bright or because they are not anxious by nature. For others, even the first spelling test is a matter of great stress. They may be perfectionists, or perhaps they simply do not handle pressure well. Whatever way your child approaches exams or tests, your support and love are vital. Children who know that they are loved and that their talents are appreciated will learn to cope well with exams and to seek help from you if they are worried.

Part of the stress about the Leaving Certificate has to do with the fact that it and other state exams are recognised as standards of achievement for young people applying for third-level places or for jobs. In the period leading up to the exam, the routines established for study and the support of parents will help to ensure that the child is not overwhelmed. It is important that parents do not increase anxiety by pushing too hard, making demands that the young person cannot meet or expecting her to get the same or better results than another family member.

If you feel your son or daughter is becoming too anxious about exams, is losing sleep, having nightmares, not eating regularly or is not able to concentrate, talk to them about what is happening. Make sure that they have enough exercise and leisure time. If you are worried, consult their teachers.

Most young people are very conscious of the need to do well in exams. The points system for college entry leaves them in no doubt about what they have to achieve. However, if they know that you appreciate them for doing their best and that you want them to feel content, and if you have always helped them to think through their options, then the pressure can help them to do well. They will not want to let you down, so it is important that they understand that you love them for what they can do.

Problems at school

If a child is unhappy at school or complains about some aspect of school life it is essential to check with the teacher or school principal to try to find out what they think is the trouble. Most schools welcome the involvement of parents, but things can still go wrong. Listen to what your child says if he seems worried or upset by something at school. Then listen to the teacher before deciding what to do. Never jump to conclusions. The child who insists that he is being picked on by a teacher could be right, but it could be that the teacher has had to deal with disruption in class. Some schools may not suit certain children. Even after careful selection, the school may not be right for your child.

Truanting

Most of us know this as mitching and we probably mitched once, or at least made complex plans for a day at the pictures or walking round town! Mitching once, for the adventure or perhaps as a dare, is one thing, but young people who miss school regularly or even for whole terms are a serious problem.

It can be difficult for schools to monitor attendance after a morning roll call, so we really do not know the extent of the problem. Frequent truancy not only results in lost time in class but can suggest a deeper problem; it has been called the kindergarten of crime.

If your child is mitching frequently, do not ignore the problem, hoping that it will resolve itself. Commonsense and a good relationship with your child and the teachers at the school should ensure that you get to the root of any difficulties quickly. You must find out why, and whether your child is doing it alone or in a group.

Ask the school to notify you immediately if your child is absent.

Summer holidays

The long summer holidays can be a big strain on the family, especially if both parents are working outside the home. We often feel that young people have too much time on their hands, too much freedom and too many opportunities to get into trouble.

Try looking at summer holidays as an opportunity for your son or daughter to pursue a new hobby or interest. Many teenagers go to summer camps or take language courses. Older teenagers may be able to work part-time or do a course that they could not take at school.

Knowing where your adolescents are, agreeing when they should be home and encouraging them to invite their friends back to the house are still important. As your teenagers get older and the rules can begin to be extended, holiday times are an opportunity to allow the odd late night because there is no school the next morning.

It is worth remembering that teenagers are almost adults and should share most household duties. They should enjoy their free time, but not while you are slaving over the cooker, washing machine or iron. Women need to be especially conscious of not simply continuing patterns of care when their children are well able to do things for themselves.

Being a parent of teenagers is both rewarding and exasperating. There are days when you feel that you are raising a well-balanced, happy and co-operative human being; on others, you wonder where you went wrong. The most important things you can show are commonsense, genuine respect for your children, fairness and flexibility. You want your children to become adults who can think for themselves and manage their own lives. This process begins as they challenge your values and your views of the world. The more positively you see this challenge, the more you will enjoy your child's adolescence.

Some useful tips

- Praise your children regularly, from the earliest age.
- Encourage them, as they get older, to be aware of your need for praise too.
- In the case of families with young children, try to establish a separate 'adult only' time by adhering to a regular bedtime routine. Use this time to touch base with your partner or friends — don't spend it doing housework, etc!
- Cut down on the amount of choice you offer to your children. Avoid asking 'What would you like?'. Instead, try 'You may have this or that'.
- Try not to make any negative comments (even in jest) about your children's choice of clothes, hairstyle, etc.
- Encourage your children's friends to visit your home regularly, and provide snacks and goodies on occasions. You will get to know them in this way.
- Keep in touch with other parents, and let your children know of this.
- Do not be drawn into your children's squabbles. They will do their best to involve you, but try changing your tactics and ignore or pretend to ignore their behaviour. Watch the change!
- Try to avoid language like 'You should have done this' or 'You never do this or that'. Try instead an approach like 'I would be happier if you didn't do this or that'.
- Try not to repeat with your children the behaviour or comments that irritated or hurt *you* as a child.
- If your job is getting you down, try not to pass on the worry of it to your children. They will not understand.
- If there is a family crisis, remember to reassure your children that it is over when it is over. Children, especially teenagers, often go on worrying unnecessarily.

- If your partner and yourself do not get along, both parents should reassure the child that it is not his/her fault.
- Keep in touch with school and after-school activities.
- Listen to and try to *understand* what your children are saying.
- Do not be afraid to show your emotions and to explain a problem as you see it, rather than as you feel your child *should* see it.
- Be genuine when you praise your children.
- Make time to meet with groups of friends, neighbours and family, with whom you can exchange child-minding.
- Encourage your children to take responsibility for their own decisions (within the bounds of safety).
- Dismiss teenagers' lack of interest in you or in other family members. It is less real than you imagine, and it will pass.
- Don't scold children or teenagers in front of their friends — deal with the problem later on when calmness has returned.
- Try to establish a pattern of family meetings where everyone gets their say and where decisions are made and then adhered to by everyone.
- Try to ask your child specific questions rather than general ones, for example, 'Did Miss Murphy like your essay?' rather than 'How was school today?'.
- Assume that your teenager has had a cigarette or a drink at some stage. Be firm in your own ground rules and trust your own example.
- Your teenagers are at a level of heightened sexual awareness. Be aware of it and be prepared to engage in open and honest discussion.
- Imagine your young teenagers canoeing through calm waters until suddenly they hit the rapids and have to fend entirely for themselves in order to survive. This may help you to understand how they feel as they go through the turmoil of the teenage years.

Directory of services for families

The majority of the organisations listed here are Dublin-based. However, many do have local branches throughout the country. For information on countrywide services, please contact the addresses/telephone numbers listed or, alternatively, consult Directory Enquiries.

Telephone numbers and addresses are liable to change. If in doubt, check with Directory Enquiries. Similarly, opening hours and other such details can change, so you are advised to check before making arrangements.

Directory Index

Directory of Services for Families

(excluding services provided by the Health Boards)

A

Abortion

Women Hurt by Abortion
8, Upper Dorset St, Dublin 1

Network of caring confidential groups providing an approach to healing for women who have had an abortion.
Ballinasloe (0905) 42483; Cork (021) 883373; Drogheda (041) 31510; Dublin (01) 211151; Dundalk (042) 39638; Galway (091) 22845; Limerick (061) 339245; Mullingar (044) 41735; Portlaoise (0502) 22609; Sligo (071) 69059; Tralee (066) 25462; Waterford (051) 98120.

Challenge
Sion House, Sion Rd, Kilkenny
Tel: (056) 21653/61201

Post-abortion counselling available. (See *Unmarried Parent* for other services offered by Challenge.)

Dublin Well Woman Centre
60, Eccles St, Dublin 7
73, Lower Leeson St, Dublin 2
Tel: (01) 728051/610083/610086

Post-abortion counselling available. (See *Family Planning* for other services offered by Well Woman.)

Accommodation (See *Homeless*)

Adolescence

Teen Counselling
37, Greenfort Gardens, Clondalkin, Dublin 22.
Tel: (01) 6231398
Clondalkin and Lucan areas only.

An extension of Mater Dei Adolescent Counselling Centre, Clonliffe Road. Offers counselling to young people, aged 12 to 16 approx., where there are family problems; problems relating to alcohol or drugs, behavioural or emotional problems. For both young people and parents.
Referral from: school counsellors, social workers, GPs, drug counsellors, parents, youth workers, junior liaison officers, clergy, etc.

Drinking
Mary Ellen McCann, Youth Action Group, Ballymun
Tel: (01) 428071

Fr Paul Andrews
Tel: (01) 682739
Provides counselling for teenagers with a wide range of problems.

Adoption

If you decide you want to adopt a child, you should first contact an adoption agency, of which there are about twenty throughout the country. The Adoption Board, Hawkins Street, Dublin 20, will supply a list.

Barnardo's Adoption Advice Service
244, Harold's Cross Rd, Dublin 6
Tel: (01) 977276 (Tues. 2-6.30 pm)
This is *not* an adoption agency but will provide helpful guidance through their confidential phone-in service. Interviews are by appointment.

Adoptive Parents Association of Ireland
17, Clyde Rd, Ballsbridge, Dublin 4
Tel: (01) 682685
Advice on adoption matters. Aims to seek improvements in existing adoption legislation and practices where necessary.

Challenge
Sion House, Sion Rd., Kilkenny
Tel: (056) 21653/61210
Registered Adoption Society. Post-adoption counselling service available.

St Patrick's Guild
Mother and Child Welfare Agency and Adoption Service
82, Haddington Rd, Dublin 4
Tel: (01) 691908/681765
Organises adoption placement, offers post-adoption counselling for adopters and adoptees.
(See also *Unmarried Parent* and *Pregnancy/Maternity*)

Aged (See Elderly)

Agoraphobia

Out and About Association
St John's House, Seafield Rd, Clontarf, Dublin 3
Tel: (01) 338252/332003
Aims to help people who suffer from agoraphobia. Self-help support groups meet in Galway, Cork, Sligo, Dublin, to allow sufferers to make personal contact with other sufferers and to educate relatives regarding their role in helping recovery.

AIDS

Aids Helpline Cork
Tel: (021) 276676
Information service on AIDS and other health matters, provided by Gay Health Action Cork.

Aids Helpline Dublin
Tel: (01) 724277
This is an anonymous telephone help-line. Ring for hours of service.

Cairde — Body Positive Support Group
189/193 Parnell St, Dublin 1
Tel: (01) 733799
Telephone service, befriending service, one-to-one contact if required. Support groups organised. Initial contact by phone or letter.

Dublin Well Woman Centre
60, Eccles St, Dublin 7
73, Lr Leeson St, Dublin 2
Tel: (01) 302626/28052/610083/610086
Offers HIV testing and counselling. (For other services offered see *Family Planning*.)

Women and Aids
P.O. Box 1884, Sheriff St, Dublin 1
Information and resource group for women concerned with AIDS. Regular meetings.

Alcoholism

Al Anon Family Groups
Al Anon Information Centre, 19, Fleet St, Dublin 2
Tel: (01) 774195
Fellowship of men and women whose lives have been or are being affected by another person's compulsive drinking.

Alateen
Al Anon Information Centre, 19, Fleet St, Dublin 2
Tel: (01) 774195
A fellowship of young people whose lives have been or are being affected by parents' compulsive drinking.

Alcoholics Anonymous
109, St Circular Rd, Leonard's Corner, Dublin 8
Tel: (01) 538998/537677
Fellowship of men and women alcoholics.

Alcoholic Rehabilitation Centre
Goldenbridge House, Inchicore, Dublin 8
Tel: (01) 543793
Rehabilitation of alcoholics and counselling service.

Cuan Mhuire Rehabilitation Centre
Athy, Co. Kildare; Newry, Co. Down; Bruree, Co. Limerick
Tel: (0507) 31493/31564

Rehabilitation of alcoholics and drug addicts.

Dublin Central Mission
7, Marlborough Place, Dublin 1
Tel: (01) 742123

Day facilities for those with alcohol-related problems.

Hanley Centre
The Mews, Eblana Ave, Dun Laoghaire, Co. Dublin
Tel: (01) 809795/807269

Confidential information and counselling for those whose lives are being affected by a drinking problem.

Rutland Centre Ltd
Knocklyon House, Knocklyon Rd, Templeogue, Dublin 16
Tel: (01) 946761/946358/946972

Provides assessment, drug-free residential and family treatment, and structural follow-up for males and females, aged 17 upwards, who are addicted to alcohol, drugs or gambling.

Shelter Referral
288, Merrion Rd, Dublin 4
Tel: (01) 691686

Operates the Merrion Centre rehabilitation programme for alcoholics. This residential day programme caters for up to ten men. Service includes work and social skills, counselling and group therapy, with AA participation.

Alzheimer's Disease

Alzheimer's Society of Ireland
St John of God, Stillorgan, Co. Dublin
Tel: (01) 881282

Aims to arouse awareness, to supply information and literature, to establish branches and support groups throughout the country, to press all relevant authorities to recognise the scale of the problem, and to support medical and social research into the causes and incidence of Alzheimer's Disease. Branches in Dublin, Cork, Galway and Limerick.

Anorexia

Overeaters Anonymous for All Eating Disorders
Tel: (01) 694800, ext. 250

Provides self-help for those suffering from eating disorders. Meetings countrywide, following 12-step recovery programme.

Arthritis

Arthritis Foundation of Ireland
1, Clanwilliam Sq, Grand Canal Quay, Dublin 2
Tel: (01) 618188

Raises money for further research, education and patient care.

Arthritis Youth (under-35 group)
1, Clanwilliam Sq, Grand Canal Quay, Dublin 2
Tel: (01) 618188

A support group for young people with arthritis.

Asthma

Asthma Society of Ireland
24, Anglesea St, Dublin 2
Tel: (01) 716551

Provides an information service. Holds meetings, exhibitions. Runs weekly swimming sessions in Dublin and in some provincial centres. Organises holiday scheme and acts as pressure group. Local branches.

Autism

Irish Society for Autistic Children
14, Lower O'Connell St, Dublin 1
Tel: (01) 744686

Provides support and services for autistic children and adults. Runs special school and community for autistic adults in Co. Kildare.

Gheel Training Group Ltd
Milltown Therapeutic Centre, Milltown Rd, Dublin 6
Tel: (01) 698148/697405

Aims to provide life-long caring and developmental service, both day and residential, for autistic adults. Social training centre, sheltered workshop and three hostels in the Dublin area.

B

Battered Women/Men (Also see *Homeless*)

Adapt
Adapt House, Rosbrien, Limerick
Tel: (061) 42354/42950

Provides shelter and support to battered women and their children. Counselling and information by phone.

Cuanlee
Kyrl's Quay, Cork
Tel: (021) 277698

Hostel for battered wives, referred by organisations or who contact hostel themselves.

Family Law Action Group
Tel: (01) 411607

Can assist women in securing a barring order (within 24 hours in urgent cases).

Women's Aid
P.O. Box 791, Dublin 6
Tel: (01) 961002/971370

Refuge for women and children who have to leave home because of violence by their partners. Provides them with the information and support necessary to rebuild their lives.

Bereavement

Bereavement Counselling Service
P.O. Box 1508, Dublin 8
Tel: (01) 767727

Centre for counselling: St Anne's Church, Dawson St, Dublin 2

Bereavement Society
c/o Siobhán Savage, Magheraboy, Carrickmacross, Co. Monaghan
Tel: (042) 62341

Self-help group of bereaved people who meet regularly to share their grief. Aims to help newly-bereaved cope with their grief, to make society aware of the needs of the bereaved. Professional back-up available. Confidential.

Irish Stillbirth and Neonatal Death Society
P.O. Box 2475, Swords, Co. Dublin
Tel: (01) 859791/809163/831919

Group of parents who have experienced the loss of a baby around the time of birth, and are willing to befriend and support other bereaved families.

Irish Sudden Infant Death Association
Carmichael House, Nth Brunswick St, Dublin 7
Tel: (01) 747007

Aims to help and support parents bereaved by sudden infant death (cot death) and to raise funds for research. Organises meetings, seminars, disseminates information. 24-hour telephone help-line. One to one, couple-to-couple befriending service. Drop-in centre for bereaved families.

Birth Control (See *Family Planning*)

Blind/Visually Impaired

Board for the Employment of the Blind
Ardee Rd, Rathmines, Dublin 6
Tel: (01) 9766633

Provides employment for 50 registered blind and 20 sighted workers in its workshops at Rathmines. Trades as Irish Blindcraft and retails through its own showroom at 121 Lr Rathmines Rd.

Irish Guide Dogs Association
Training Centre, Model Farm Rd, Cork
Tel: (021) 870929

Promotes freedom and mobility for the blind and visually impaired, through the supply of trained guide dogs. Provides training in orientation and mobility skills and the use of the long cane.

National Council for the Blind of Ireland
Doyle House, 45, Whitworth Rd, Drumcondra, Dublin 9
Tel: (01) 307033

Social workers cover the twenty-six counties.

National League of the Blind of Ireland
35, Gardiner Place, Dublin 1
Tel: (01) 742792/745827

This is a registered trade union. It has a comprehensive welfare programme and operates a day-care centre for elderly blind people.

Brain Injuries (See also *Mentally Handicapped*)

Headway
c/o 13, Stradbrook Lawn, Blackrock, Co. Dublin
Tel: (01) 806623/908784/823643

The association meets every month when members, comprising those who have had a head injury, their families and the professionals can exchange ideas, attitudes and experiences relating to head injury.

Irish Society for Brain-Injured Children
Kinacourt House, Portarlington, Co. Laois
Tel: (0502) 23139

Provides treatment facilities for brain-injured children, through home rehabilitation programmes. Runs Diagnostic Evaluation and Treatment Centre.

Breast-feeding

La Leche League
P.O. Box 1280, Raheny, Dublin 5
Tel: (01) 463248/(051) 55784

Helps mothers who want to breast-feed their babies. Local groups and individual counsellors (see Telephone Directory) offer information, leaflets, books, and informal gatherings for mothers.

Bullying

Campaign Against Bullying
72, Lakelands Ave, Kilmacud, Stillorgan
Tel: (01) 887976

Offers support to parents whose children are being bullied at school.

C

Cancer

Comfort For Cancer
16, Southdene, Monkstown Valley, Co. Dublin
Tel: (01) 843276

A support group for cancer patients and their families. Aims to give comfort to those touched in any way by the illness by holding meetings to share a common experience, exchange letters and telephone calls.

Helpful Hands
124, Meadowvale, Blackrock, Co. Dublin
Tel: (01) 892163/895758

Provides help with home-care, mainly for cancer patients, and support for their caring relatives.

Irish Cancer Society
5, Northumberland Rd, Dublin 4
Tel: (01) 681855

Provides funds for research, welfare and information concerning cancer. Organises 'Reach to Recovery' programmes for mastectomy patients (see below). Information and advice available to Ostomy, Hodgkin's Disease and Laryngectomy patients. Provides cash grants to needy cancer patients, endows hospital beds for terminal cancer patients, and supports limited home nursing service. Freephone information and support service.
'Reach to Recovery': Supportive programme for women who are about to have or have recently had breast surgery. Phone-in advice and support service. Dial 10 and ask the operator for Cancer Freefone — a free countryside service.

Turning Point
Tel: (01) 602600

The centre offers a holistic health programme, complementary to orthodox medicine, involving: support and therapeutic groups, autogenics, diet education and counselling with individuals, couples and families. Aimed at those experiencing life crises such as severe illness, and cancer in particular.

Cerebral Palsy

National Association
Sandymount Avenue
Dublin 4
Tel: (01) 695355

Offers interdisciplinary team assessments and treatments, nurseries and pre-schools, special national schools and boarding schools, sports, pre-vocational and leisure training for children with developmental delay and physical disabilities. For severely physically disabled adults, vocational training, sheltered work and/or day activity services are available. Branches throughout the country.

Child Guidance Centres

Castleknock Child and Family Centre
Dublin 15
Tel: (01) 214385

Referrals: GP, area medical officer

Child and Family Centre
Ballyfermot Rd, Dublin 10
Tel: (01) 6267511/6265676

Referrals: GP, area medical officer, social worker
Health Board area: 5

Child Guidance Clinic
Mater Hospital
Tel: (01) 300700

Referrals: GP, school, social worker, self-referral
Health Board areas: 7, 8

Cluain Mhuire
Blackrock
Tel: (01) 800365

Medical referrals only, for ages 6-12, 12-20, 20 + .

Dept of Child Psychiatry
1, James's St, Dublin 8
Tel: (01) 543710/537951

Referrals: GP, school, social worker
Health Board areas: 5, 6

Mater Child and Family Centre
7, Towers Centre, Ballymun Social Centre
Tel: (01) 420622/420809/420319
Referrals: GP, school, social worker, self-referral

Mater Dei
(Eastern Health Board), Clonliffe Rd, Dublin 3
Tel: (01) 371892
No referral necessary

St John of God
Family Centre, Tallaght, Dublin 24
Tel: (01) 515447
Health Board area: 4

St John of God
Orwell Rd, Rathgar, Dublin 6
Tel: (01) 977596
Referrals: GP, school.
Health Board areas: 1, 2, 3, 4

Child-Line Service

Child-Line
c/o ISPCC
Freephone service
Tel: (01) 6793333
Children can talk to a trained volunteer on any subject.

Children in Care (Also see Fostering)

Parents of Children in Care
c/o Gingerbread, 12, Wicklow St, Dublin 2
Tel: (01) 710291
Support group meets last Monday of every month at 8.00 pm.

Children in Hospital

Association for the Welfare of Children in Hospital
c/o Brookwood, Tubber, Lucan, Co. Dublin
Tel: (01) 889278
Aims to educate parents and hospitals on the needs of sick children and to improve visiting, play and other facilities. Gives practical advice to parents.

Coeliac Disorders

Coeliac Society of Ireland
Carmichael House, Nth Brunswick St, Dublin 7
Tel: (01) 721233

Aims to protect and safeguard interests of members relating to the coeliac condition. Provides advice, information on diet, etc.

Colostomy

Ileostomy Association of Sth Ireland Division
278, Greenfield, Maynooth, Co. Kildare
Tel: (01) 285968

Aims to help people who have had, or are about to have, an Ileostomy/Colostomy operation to return to a fully active and normal life. Organises hospital/home visits by volunteers who have fully recovered.

Cot Death

Irish Sudden Infant Death Association
Carmichael House, Nth Brunswick St, Dublin 7
Tel: (01) 747007

Aims to help and support parents bereaved by sudden infant death (cot death). Drop-in centre, 24-hour phone-in, befriending service.

Counselling

Centre Care — Dublin Diocesan Social Service Centre
1a Cathedral St, Dublin 1
Tel: (01) 745441/726775

Social worker available for consultation on any personal or social problem. Support and counselling on problems in family relations, difficulties of single parents, accommodation problems, spiritual problems. Information on social welfare benefits, personal and community care services, housing, taxation, unemployment.

Clanwilliam Institute
18, Clanwilliam Tce, Grand Canal Quay, Dublin 2
Tel: (01) 761363/762881

Conducts treatment and study of the family. Provides consultation, counselling and mediation to families, couples, and individuals, including psychological evaluation for children, sex therapy and out-patient programme for alcohol-related problems.

Creative Counselling Centre
7, Park Rd, Dun Laoghaire, Co. Dublin
Tel: (01) 801671

Offers a range of counselling and psychotherapy services to individuals, groups and couples. Fee per hourly session.
The Creative Counselling Centre offers a confidential counselling and psychotherapy service at reduced cost with trainee therapists under supervision.

Family Therapy and Counselling Service
59, Ranelagh Village, Dublin 6
Tel: (01) 971188

Galway Psychological Services
Ruxton House, 35/37 Dominick St, Galway
Tel: (091) 64995

Offers a wide range of services, for children, adolescents and adults. Complete psychological and educational assessments, learning programmes, behaviour programmes, child management strategies, stress management, counselling. Special referral is not required.

Institute of Guidance Counsellors
221, Palmerstown Woods, Clover Hill, Clondalkin, Dublin 22
Tel: (01) 571320

Supports and promotes the work of guidance counsellors who work with students and parents at second and third level to promote personal, educational and vocational development through group work and individual counselling.
Administration of aptitude, intelligence, interest and personality tests. Referral of students to child-guidance clinics, etc.

Irish Association for Counselling
The Mews, Eblana Ave, Dun Laoghaire, Co. Dublin
Tel: (01) 801605

Provides a list of accredited counsellors.

Fr Paul Andrews
Tel: (01) 682739

Provides counselling for teenagers with a wide range of problems.

Cystic Fibrosis

Cystic Fibrosis
24, Lower Rathmines Rd, Dublin 6
Tel: (01) 962433/962186

Provides a domiciliary physiotherapy service to CF sufferers, sends children to Lourdes, sponsors several research projects.

D

Deaf/Hard of Hearing

Irish Deaf Society
Carmichael House, Nth Brunswick St, Dublin 7
Tel: (01) 721233

Promotes the welfare of the deaf in all situations of life. Information, counselling, interpreting services and Sign Language teaching available. Parents Association for Deaf and Hearing, Deaf Youth Association.

Irish Hard of Hearing Association
c/o St Joseph's, Brewery Rd, Stillorgan, Co. Dublin

Assists in the formation of small hard of hearing groups, counselling in relation to lip-reading, wearing of hearing aids, promotes installation of loops, etc.

National Association for the Deaf
25, Lower Leeson St, Dublin 2
Tel: (01) 763188

Social worker
Tel: (01) 762597

Aims to provide improved conditions and opportunities for the deaf and hard of hearing.

Death (See *Bereavement*)

Depression (Also see *Mental Illness*)

Aware
St Patrick's Hospital, James's St, Dublin 8
Tel: (01) 775423, ext 429

Assists and gives support to people suffering from depression and elation. Provides factual information about the disorders and supportive group therapy sessions.

Samaritans
112, Marlborough St, Dublin 1
Tel: (01) 727700

Works for the prevention of suicide, and befriends the lonely, despairing and suicidal.
CORK: Coach Street (021) 271323. ENNIS: Kilrush Road (065) 29777.
GALWAY: 14, Nun's Island (091) 61222. LIMERICK: 25, Cecil Street (061) 42111. SLIGO: 12, Capel Street (071) 42011. TRALEE: 44, Moyderwell Street (066) 22566. WATERFORD: 13, Beau Street (051) 72114

Diabetes

Irish Diabetic Association
82/83, Lower Gardiner St, Dublin 1
Tel: (01) 363022

Aims to help diabetics, through visits and meetings, and to raise money for research and for diabetic children's holidays.

Disabled Drivers

Disabled Drivers' Association
Ballindine, Co. Mayo
Tel: (094) 64266/64054

Carmichael House, Nth Brunswick St, Dublin 7
Tel: (01) 721233

Operates a Driving Assessment Centre and Driving School. Provides aids and adaptations for cars.

Down's Syndrome

Down's Syndrome Association
27, South William St, Dublin 2
Tel: (01) 793322/79763

Aims to make available to parents and guardians information to assist them in helping Down's Syndrome persons develop to their full potential. The association is organised on a county basis.

Cork branch: C/o Mary Twohig, Gortnalee, Carrignaver, Co. Cork
Tel: (021) 884295

Drugs

Coolmine Therapeutic Community
19, Lord Edward St, Dublin, 2
Tel: (01) 793765/782300

Offers drug abusers the opportunity to learn to live without drugs through self-help.

Cuan Mhuire Rehabilitation Centre
Athy, Co. Kildare; Newry, Co. Down; Bruree, Co. Limerick
Tel: (0507) 31493/31564

Rehabilitation of alcoholics and drug addicts.

Drug Unit, Beaumont Hospital
Tel: (01) 379964/379966

Dun Laoghaire Drugs Awareness Group
Tel: (01) 803728

Drugs Counsellor
Health Centre, Patrick Street, Dun Laoghaire
Tel: (01) 808461

Drug Treatment Centre Board
Trinity Court, 30/31 Pearse St, Dublin 2
Tel: (01) 771122

Help for drug dependants as out-patients or in-patients. No referral needed.
Treatment free. Advisory service to parents, young people, teachers, etc.

Families Anonymous
Community Centre, Church of St Therese, Mount Merrion, Dublin 14
Tel: (01) 902146

Aims to help relatives and friends of people involved in drug abuse. Weekly
meetings. Exchange of members' phone numbers.

Garda Síochána Drug Squad
Castle Yard, Dublin 2.
Tel: (01) 651356/73222

Nar-Anon
c/o 38, Gardiner St, Dublin 1

Fellowship for those affected by another's involvement with drugs.

Narcotics Anonymous
13, Talbot St, Dublin 1
Tel: (01) 300944, ext 486

Aims to help drug addicts recover from addiction. 24-hour telephone
answering service. Regular meetings where members help each other to stay
clean and to recover from addiction.

Rutland Centre Ltd
Knocklyon House, Knocklyon Rd, Templeogue, Dublin 16
Tel: (01) 946358/946972/946761

Provides assessment, drug-free residential and family treatment, and
structural follow-up for persons aged 17 upwards who are addicted to drugs,
alcohol or gambling.

Dyslexia

Irish Assoc. for Children and Adults with Learning Disabilities
27, Upper Mount St, Dublin 2
Tel: (01) 611826 (mornings)

Aims to secure adequate diagnostic facilities and early remedial tuition for
people with specific difficulties in reading, writing and/or arithmetic.

E

Eating Disorders

Overeaters Anonymous
Tel: (01) 694800, ext. 250

Provides self-help for those suffering from *all* eating disorders.

Eczema

National Eczema Society
43, Galtymore, Rd, Drimnagh, Dublin 12
Tel: (01) 557807

Provides support and information for eczema sufferers and their parents.

Education (See also *Psychologist*)

Adult Education Organisers' Association
Tel: (056) 22165

Promotes the development of adult education.
Contact: County Adult Education Officer, Vocational School, Ormonde Rd, Kilkenny.

Alternative Education for Young People
Tel: (01) 680614

The phone no. given is Dublin City VEC, where information can be obtained on projects available.

Dun Laoghaire: Tivoli Road. (Tel: 01-841028)
FÁS involvement, participants receive an allowance. Children who have had contact with the courts are involved with this project.

Dun Laoghaire: York Rd. (Tel: 01-808638)
Similar to above, but Dept of Justice not involved.

Aontas, National Association for Adult Education
65, Fitzwilliam Sq, Dublin 2
Tel: (01) 610571

Promotes the development of adult education, and can supply information on courses etc.

Dublin Institute of Adult Education
1/3 Mountjoy Sq, Dublin 1
Tel: (01) 787266

Provides adult education courses and develops community adult education programmes in association with local groups.

Dublin Literary Scheme
1/3 Mountjoy Sq, Dublin 1
Tel: (01) 745277

Trained tutors. Arranges one-to-one tuition. Assists local groups.

National Adult Literacy Agency
8, Gardiner Place, Dublin 1
Tel: (01) 787205

Promotes and develops adult literacy work. Provides information and advice.
Resource centre, training and research available. Organises seminars, meetings
and workshops.

Elderly (Also see *Pensioners* and *Retirement*)

Carers Association
68, Gt Strand St, Dublin 1
Tel: (01) 727666

Aims to represent the relatives who provide care for the elderly at home,
by providing information and advice, by lobbying for services. Support
group meetings at 81, Marlboro St, Dublin 1.

Friends of the Elderly
25, Bolton St, Dublin 1
Tel: (01) 731146/731855/731267

Services include social work, home and hospital visits, transport, minor home
improvements, holidays, outings and parties.

Emigration

Action Group for Irish Youth
5-15 Cromer St, London WC1 H8LS
Tel: London 278-1665

Aims to promote the interests and welfare of young Irish emigrants in
London.

Emigrant Advice
1a Cathedral St, Dublin 1
Tel: (01) 732844

Provides an information and counselling service for intending emigrants in
order that they can make an informed, responsible decision about emigrating.

Epilepsy

Irish Epilepsy Association
249, Crumlin Rd, Dublin 12
Tel: (01) 557500

Social work service, education, advisory service. Aims to encourage and assist
research into the causes and treatment of epilepsy, and to promote awareness
of the need for education and rehabilitation.

F

Family Mediation

Family Mediation Service
Irish Life Centre, Lr Abbey St, Dublin 1
Tel: (01) 728277/728475/728708

Operated under the auspices of the Dept of Justice. The aim is to help couples who have decided to separate to negotiate their own separation terms, and to work out mutually acceptable arrangements on such matters as parenting the children, maintenance and family home and property. The objective is to prevent matters going to the courts. This *is not* marriage counselling. The service is free.

Family Planning

Catholic Marriage Advisory Council (CMAC)
All Hallows College, Dublin 9
Tel: (01) 375649/371151

There are fifty-five centres throughout Ireland (see Telephone Directory for numbers). The following services are available: pre-marriage preparation courses; counselling service for those experiencing difficulties in their relationships; information on all methods of family planning and instruction in natural methods; marital sexual therapy for couples experiencing sexual difficulties in the marriage relationship.

Couple to Couple League
Box 1869, Dublin 16
Tel: (01) 947400

Aims to build healthy marriages through natural family planning and to carry out religious and civic education in matters of family life. Encourages breast-feeding, and is active in the fields of infertility and pre-menstrual tension. Runs courses for couples. Phone for details of fees.

Dublin Well Woman Centre
60, Eccles St, Dublin 7
Tel: (01) 728051

73, Lower Leeson St, Dublin 2
Tel: (01) 610083/610086

Advice, help and counselling. Service provided on methods of contraception, sterilisation and vasectomy.
The Well Woman Centre also offers the following services:
Donor-insemination; mail order for sexual aids; menopause and hormone replacement therapy (HRT) clinics; cervical and breast examination; rubella screening; mother and baby clinic; assertiveness training; bereavement and stress-related counselling; infertility clinics; HIV test and counselling; post-abortion counselling; PMT clinics; remedial and shiatsu massage; yoga classes; acupuncture. Costs vary.

Family Planning Services Ltd
Clinics: 67 Pembroke Rd, Dublin 4
Tel: (01) 681108

78a/79 Lr Georges St, Dun Laoghaire
Tel: (01) 841666

Medical clinics: all methods of contraception (pill, cap, IUD, Billings and natural methods); counselling for psycho-sexual, pre-menstrual and menopausal problems. Pregnancy testing and vasectomies are also carried out. Family planning teams consisting of doctors and nurses are available for in-house smear-testing and breast examination.
Contraceptive supplies: non-medical contraceptives and literature are available to callers and by post.

Irish Family Planning Association
15, Mountjoy Sq, Dublin 1
Tel: (01) 740723/744133

Provides a comprehensive contraceptive and women's health service, including special services for women suffering from pre-menstrual syndrome or the menopause. A confidential postal service is also available.
The Association runs sex education courses for professionals and parents and provides speakers and audio-visual material for youth and women's groups.
Their Book Centre has a wide selection of books on family planning, relationships, sexual problems, women's health and sex education.
Youth Group: The IFPA also provides informed peer group education in the areas of sexuality and relationships, and makes information available about young people and sexuality in Ireland. A confidential telephone service for adolescents also operates.

National Association of the Ovulation Method of Ireland
16, North Great Georges St, Dublin 1
Tel: (01) 786156

36, Washington St, Cork
Tel: (021) 272213

Aims to teach and promote natural family planning (the ovulation method — Billings) to engaged and married couples. Organises Engaged Couples Courses, public talks on menopause, infertility, sub-fertility and the philosophy of natural family planning.
Approximately eighty-seven centres in Ireland. A postal service is available to cater for unserviced areas.
Initial small subscription.

Family Therapy (Also see *Counselling*)

Clanwilliam Institute
18, Clanwilliam Tce, Grand Canal Quay, Dublin 2
Tel: (01) 761363/762881

Offers a wide range of professional services to individuals, couples and families with concerns such as: children's behaviour and development; marriage difficulties; sexual problems; problems associated with alcohol and drug abuse; chronic illness and bereavement; anxiety, depression, phobias and stress.
Referral is not required. Appointment may be requested by phone or in writing, and can usually be arranged within a week.
Fees: A sliding scale of fees is operated with the amount agreed at or before the first session and being payable at each session.

Fostering

Barnardo's
244/246, Harolds' Cross, Dublin 6W
Tel: (01) 977276/977313

Day foster-care and day nursery in Dun Laoghaire. Community projects and day nurseries in Tallaght, Mulhuddart, Blanchardstown and Ballybrack. Community project in Fatima Mansions.

Challenge
Sion House, Sion Rd, Kilkenny
Tel: (056) 21653/61210

Offers foster-care for limited period. Help with day-care. Befriending service for women keeping their babies. Counselling and support services for single parents and their families.

Irish Foster Care Association
60, Grange Wood, Rathfarnham, Dublin 16
Tel: (01) 944229

Provides information and counselling. Liaises with Health Boards. Promotes the welfare of children in care.

G

Gambling

Alcoholic Rehabilitation Centre
Goldenbridge House, Inchicore, Dublin 8
Tel: (01) 543793

Offers counselling for those with gambling addictions.

Gam-Anon
Carmichael House, Nth Brunswick St, Dublin 7
Tel: (01) 721133

Aims to help families of compulsive gamblers to understand the gambling addiction, and how to overcome problems. Organises group therapy, telephone contact, advice.

Gamblers Anonymous
Carmichael House, Nth Brunswick St, Dublin 7
Tel: (01) 721133

10.30am-4.30pm, Mon-Fri
Support for those who desire to stop gambling. Regular meetings. Can arrange personal contact.

Rutland Centre Ltd
Tel: (01) 946358/946972/946761

Provides assessment and family treatment, and structural follow-up for persons aged 17 upwards who are addicted to gambling, alcohol and drugs. Residential service available.

Garda Síochána

Garda Síochána Juvenile Liaison Officer
Harcourt Sq, Harcourt St, Dublin 2
Tel: (01) 732222, ext 303/305

There are liaison officers in most areas. These are plain clothes gardaí who deal with first offenders aged between 7 and 17, and occasionally, on request, with others. The aim is to dispose of cases outside the courts through a caution. Assistance will also be given to parents to help them in the prevention of crime — information given will not go on official garda files. Contact can be made through the above phone numbers if caller prefers not to use the local station.

Gay

Gay Health Action
Tel: (01) 531165
P.O. Box 1890, Sheriff St, Dublin 1

Offers an AIDS telephone information service. Aims to provide clear and accurate information on AIDS and related issues.

Gay Information Cork
24, Sullivan's Quay, Cork
Tel: (021) 317026

Information service for gay men. Operates 7-9.00 pm Wednesdays.

Gay Switchboard (Tell-a-Friend)
Carmichael House, Nth Brunswick St, Dublin 7
Tel: (01) 721055

Counselling, support and information for gay people and bi-sexuals. Also Parents' Inquiry Service.
'Ice Breakers': Service through the Gay Switchboard to help gays 'coming out'.

Gay Youth Group
Hirschfield Centre, 10 Fownes St, Dublin 2
Tel: (01) 710939

Organises meetings, social events etc for the under-25s to help young people to meet each other.

Irish Family Planning Association
Tel: (01) 744133/740723

Offers a confidential help-line for people concerned about their sexuality.

National Gay Federation
Hirschfield Centre, 10 Fownes St, Dublin 2
Tel: (01) 710939

Provides a centre for gay organisations. Publishes 'Gay Community News' monthly.

Gifted Children

Irish Association for Gifted Children
Carmichael House, Nth Brunswick St, Dublin 7
Tel: (01) 721233

Aims to assist parents, educators and the social services in the care of gifted and talented children in Ireland. Holds seminars for parents and teachers, activities for gifted children. Telephone counselling available.

H

Haemophilia

Irish Haemophilia Association
Carmichael House, Nth Brunswick St, Dublin 7
Tel: (01) 721233

Helps members with individual problems, provides information and advice. Provides counselling services for individuals who are HIV positive, emotional and financial support for patients and their families. Organises summer holidays for haemophiliac children and also regular social events. Encourages research, improvements in treatment and conditions.

Head Injuries (See *Brain Injuries*)

Health

Friends of Elizabeth Kubler-Ross
White House, Templeogue, Dublin 12

Non-profit-making organisation aimed at the promotion of physical, emotional, intellectual and spiritual health. Provides people with a safe and trusting environment to reach this goal through a programme of workshops, lectures and seminars.

Turning Point
Landsdowne Gardens, Shelbourne Rd, Dublin 4
Tel: (01) 680588/602600

Holistic health programme, complementary to orthodox medicine. Aimed at those experiencing a life crisis, such as severe illness and cancer in particular.

Heart

Irish Heart Foundation
4, Clyde Rd, Ballsbridge, Dublin 4
Tel: (01) 685001

Aim is primarily prevention of heart disease. Provides 'Mediscan' risk factor screening programme. Cardio-Pulmonary Resuscitation training courses; lectures to schools, organisations, etc.

Mended Hearts (Cardiac Support Group)
52, Bettyglen, Dublin 5
Tel: (01) 314576

A group of people who have had heart surgery, wishing to support others, and their families, who are facing surgery. Visits to hospitals where patients are awaiting heart surgery. Home visits on request. Telephone and letter communication.

Holidays

Between
'Dunlaoi', 8, North Mall, Cork
Tel: (021) 961375/275857

Organises holidays for children and families. Promotes community development and inter-community co-operation, with particular regard to Northern Ireland.

Caring and Sharing Association (CASA)
Carmichael House, Nth Brunswick St, Dublin 7
Tel: (01) 725300/725370

An organisation of voluntary helpers and handicapped people. It organises socials, outings, holiday centres in Ireland, and has an annual pilgrimage to Lourdes and Knock.

Marrowbone Lane Fund
12, College Green, Dublin 2

Provides holidays in some cases where illness, unemployment and stress are undermining family relationships.

Peacehaven Trust
Peacehaven, 1, Hillside, Greystones, Co. Wicklow
Tel: (01) 875977

Runs a family-type home for mildly and moderately mentally handicapped adults. Room available for temporary residents wishing to stay for a week or two.

Society of St Vincent de Paul

Organises holidays. Contact local branch for information (see Telephone Directory).

Home Care

National Association of Home Care Organisers
Kilbarrack Health Centre, Dublin 2
Tel: (01) 391221

Association of those who arrange home help/care for those in the community who need it. Provides information, liaison, training. Aims to promote improved service.

Homeless

Adapt
Adapt House, Rosbrien, Limerick
Tel: (061) 42354/42950

Provides shelter and support to battered women and their children. Also counselling and information by phone.

Catholic Social Service Conference
The Red House, Clonliffe College, Dublin 3
Tel: (01) 360011/5

Provides a wide range of social services. Hostel accommodation for young boys at risk. Enquiries also to Centre Care, Cathedral St, Dublin 1.

Cheshire Foundation of Ireland
20a, Herbert Lane, Dublin 2
Tel: (01) 614550/761058

Provides residential accommodation for the care, nursing and general well-being of people, regardless of creed, who are chronically ill or permanently disabled, especially those of limited means.

Cuanlee
Kyrl's Quay, Cork
Tel: (021) 277698

Hostel for battered wives, referred by organisations or may contact hostel themselves.

Focus Point
14A, Eustace St, Dublin 2
Tel: (01) 712555

Provides a housing information, advice and settlement service to people who have severe accommodation problems, or who are 'out-of-home'. Drop-in, low-cost coffee shop and night centre, centre of alternatives for young people. Home-making service and nursery; supportive housing project for young women; residential, educational and leisure centre.

House a Marriage
St Francis Xavier's Social Service Centre, 28 Upr Sherrard St, Dublin 1
Tel: (01) 740439

Aims to provide flatlets at nominal rents to young married couples to enable them to save for their own homes.

Interaid
33, Oaktree Rd, Stillorgan, Co. Dublin
Tel: (01) 889944

Contact *only* via a social worker. Provides interim accommodation for those who are socially disadvantaged, while awaiting a permanent residence. Bed/sitting-room facility. Service for men and women with or without children.

Irish Council for Social Housing
The Housing Centre, 84, Merrion Sq, Dublin 2
Tel: (01) 612877

Representative and promotional federation of housing associations and voluntary organisations involved in housing services in Ireland (catering for elderly, handicapped and homeless).

Los Angeles Society
4, Conyngham Rd, Dublin 8; 22, Newtown Ave, Blackrock, Co. Dublin
Tel: (01) 774982

Provides long-term care for homeless boys. Education, employment, counselling.

Salvation Army
Le Froy House, 12/14 Eden Quay, Dublin 1
Tel: (01) 743762

Provides hostels for the homeless.

Simon Community
PO Box 1022, Lower Sheriff St, Dublin 1
Tel: (01) 711606/711319

Cares for homeless people, runs night shelters and community houses.
Centres in Cork, Dublin, Dundalk, Galway and Belfast.

Society of St Vincent de Paul
8, New Cabra Rd, Dublin 7
Tel: (01) 384164/384167/308219

Organises housing for the homeless.

Threshold
Capuchin Friary, Church St, Dublin 7
Tel: (01) 726311

Advice Centres: Dublin North (01) 726811; Dublin South (01) 964634; Cork
(021) 271250; Galway (091) 63080

Housing advice agency. Organisation dedicated to preventing homelessness,
particularly in the private rented sector. Advice and information across
housing sectors: private rented, local authority and owner occupying.

Women's Aid
P.O. Box 791, Dublin 6
Tel: (01) 961002/971370

Provides a refuge for women and children who have to leave home because
of violence by their partners; provides information and support necessary
to rebuild their lives.

Women's Refuge
1, Sillogue Rd, Ballymun
Tel: (01) 422377

24-hour service, drop-in centre. Welcomes enquiries on legal rights.
Accommodation available.

Homosexual (See *Gay*)

Hospitals (See *Children in Hospital*)

Hyperactive Children

Hyperactive Children's Support Group Ireland
4, Elton Park, Sandycove, Co. Dublin
Tel: (01) 808766

Provides help and support to the hyperactive child and its parents. Promotes
research. Hours: 8 – 10.00pm.

I

Illiteracy (See Literacy)

Impotency

Catholic Marriage Advisory Council
All Hallows' College, Dublin 9 (phone for info. on local councils)
Tel: (01) 375649/371151

Family Planning Services
67, Pembroke Rd, Dublin 4
Tel: (01) 681108
78a/79, Lr Georges St, Dun Laoghaire
Tel: (01) 841666

Irish Family Planning Association
15, Mountjoy Sq, Dublin 1
Tel: (01) 740723/744133

Well Woman Centre
60, Eccles St, Dublin
73, Lower Leeson St, Dublin 2
Tel: (01) 728051/7610083/610086

Incest (See Sexual Assault)

Infant Death

Irish Sudden Infant Death Association
Carmichael House, Nth Brunswick St, Dublin 7
Tel: (01) 747007

Aims to help and support parents bereaved by sudden infant death (cot death). 24-hour telephone help-line and information service. One-to-one, couple-to-couple befriending service. Drop-in centre for bereaved families.

Infertility (Also see Family Planning)

Infertility Support Group
c/o P.O. Box 908, 15, Mountjoy Sq, Dublin 1

Aims to provide information on causes and treatment, to set up contact systems, to represent the opinions of infertile people to health-care providers so as to improve services.

J

Juvenile Liaison Officer (See Garda Síochána)

K

Kidney Disease

Irish Kidney Association
Donor House, 156, Pembroke Rd, Ballsbridge, Dublin 4
Tel: (01) 689788/9

Twenty-two county branches for patients' support. Support group who look
after the welfare of all who suffer chronic renal failure, and sponsor research
into its causes and effects.
Prints and distributes the Kidney Donor and Multi-Organ cards. Provides
treatment facilities not provided by Health Boards or Dept of Health.
Arranges holidays (with nursing) for dialysis patients. Provides financial help
and counselling for patients and their families.

L

Law

Coolock Community Centre
Barryscourt Mall, Northside Shopping Centre, Coolock
Tel: (01) 477804/478692

Provides legal aid and advice to people in the Coolock area who cannot afford
a solicitor; holds Citizen's Rights courses.

Free Legal Aid Advice Centres (FLAC)
49, South William Street, Dublin 2
Tel: (01) 794239

FLAC runs a number of centres which provide legal advice to those unable
to afford the services of a solicitor, and gives tribunal representation for
employment and social welfare appeals.
FLAC campaigns for the introduction of a comprehensive state scheme of
legal aid for both criminal and civil matters, and examines areas of the law
that need reform.

Legal Aid
Legal Aid and Advice Centres operate in most Community Centres.
Enquiries re. times etc can be made there or by contacting FLAC.

Learning Disabilities

Irish Assoc. for Children and Adults with Learning Disabilities
(Dyslexia Association)
Tel: (01) 611826 (mornings only)

Aims to secure adequate diagnostic facilities and early remedial tuition for
people with specific difficulties in reading, writing and/or arithmetic.

Lesbian (See *Gay*)

Cork Lesbian Line Collective
c/o 24, Sullivan's Quay, Cork
Tel: (021) 317026 (Thursdays 8 – 10pm)

Provides a confidential befriending service for women.

Lesbian Line (Dublin)
c/o Council for Status of Women, 64, Lower Mount St, Dublin 2
Tel: (01) 613777 (Thursdays 7 – 10pm)

Contact, information and referral service for women questioning their
sexuality. Provides a non-directive telephone listening and information
service for women. Meets callers and introduces them to social events if
requested.

Literacy

Dublin Literacy Scheme
1/3, Mountjoy Sq, Dublin 1
Tel: (01) 745277

Information on local groups. Trains tutors, arranges one-to-one tuition,
assists local groups.

National Adult Literacy Agency
8, Gardiner Place, Dublin 1
Tel: (01) 787205

Promotes and develops adult literacy work. Information and advice on local
groups. Resource centre. Training and research available.

M

Marriage (See also Family Planning)

Catholic Marriage Advisory Council
All Hallows' College, Dublin 9
Tel: (01) 375649/371151

See Telephone Directory for all local branches. Offers pre-marriage
preparation courses; a counselling service for those experiencing difficulties
in their close relationships; information on all methods of family planning
and instruction in natural methods, and marital sexual therapy for couples
experiencing sexual difficulties in the marriage relationship.

Marriage Counselling Services Ltd
24, Grafton St, Dublin 2
Tel: (01) 720341

Provides a marriage counselling service, a sexual dysfunction clinic, marriage
preparation courses, relationship counselling, and an education service to
schools, professional groups, etc.

Mastectomy (See *Cancer*)

Menopause (See *Family Planning*)

Mental Health/Illness

Access to psychiatric services is usually by referral by the family doctor. Out-patient clinics are conducted by consultant psychiatrists at the psychiatric hospitals, at many general hospitals, and at community health centres.

Arch
8, Main St, Dundrum
Tel: (01) 500546

Recreation for mentally handicapped. Caters for leisure-time needs of teenagers and adults.

Aware
St. Patrick's Hospital, James's St, Dublin 8
Tel: (01) 775423, ext 429

Assists and gives support to people suffering from depression and elation. Provides both factual information about the disorders and supportive group therapy sessions.

Camphill Village Community
Duffcarraig, Gorey, Co. Wexford
Tel: (055) 25116
Kyle, West Callan, Co. Kilkenny
Tel: (056) 25458

Provides sheltered workshops and living accommodation for adults. Residential training for adolescents.

Caring and Sharing Association
Carmichael House, Nth Brunswick St, Dublin 7
Tel: (01) 725300/725370
Organises social outings and events, holidays centres in Ireland and annual pilgrimages to Lourdes and Knock.

Cope Foundation
Bonnongton, Montenotte, Cork
Tel: (021) 507131

Provides comprehensive services for people from Cork area who have a mental handicap, and for their families. Services include assessment clinic, pre-school, special schools, development units, vocational training units, community hostels.

Grow
50, Middle Abbey St, Dublin 1
Tel: (01) 734029
11 Liberty St, Cork
Tel: (021) 277520

Worldwide community mental health movement. Weekly meetings emphasise a self-help/mutual-help approach and the development of personal resources. Anonymous and confidential.
Drop-in centres in Dublin, Cork, Kilkenny, and Limerick.

Irish Handicapped Children's Pilgrimage Trust
7, Northumberland Ave, Dun Laoghaire, Co. Dublin
Tel: (01) 803456

Aims to bring handicapped children to Lourdes on holiday/pilgrimage for one week at Easter. Arranges after-care holidays on a regional basis.

L'Arche Community
Moorefield House, Kilmoganny, Co. Kilkenny
Tel: (051) 48049
Office: (056) 25628

'An Croi', Wilton Lawn, Wilton, Cork
Tel: (021) 546298
Office: (021) 542183

International federation of communities where people with mental handicaps and their assistants live and work together, sharing life in all its aspects.

Mental Health Association of Ireland
Mensana House, 6, Adelaide St, Dun Laoghaire, Co. Dublin
Tel: (01) 841166

Gives practical help to the mentally ill and those under stress and strain.

National Assoc. for the Mentally Handicapped of Ireland
5, Fitzwilliam Place, Dublin 2
Tel: (01) 766035

Promotes the general welfare of people with mental handicap. Central coordinating role for over 150 member organisations.

National Federation of Arch Clubs
74, Meadow Grove, Dublin 16
Tel: (01) 951081

Provides recreational facilities for people with mental handicap, at weekly social clubs.

Peacehaven Trust
Peacehaven, 1, Hillside, Greystones, Co. Wicklow
Tel: (01) 875977

Family-type home for mildly and moderately mentally handicapped adults. One room kept for temporary residents on a weekly basis.

Recovery Inc.
42, Raymond St, South Circular Rd, Dublin 8
Tel: (01) 535633

Offers self-help aftercare to prevent chronicity in nervous patients and relapses in former mental patients. Holds weekly meetings at 24 outlets.

Schizophrenia Association of Ireland
4, Fitzwilliam Place, Dublin 2
Tel: (01) 761988

Offers a confidential counselling and information service, structured system of support, guidance and mutual help for sufferers and their families. Local support groups and branches.

St Michael's House
Willowfield Park, Goatstown, Dublin 14
Tel: (01) 987033

Forty-four centres in Dublin area. Aims to assist people with mental handicap and their families by running day centres, schools, clinics, workshops, community hostels and group homes.

Union of Voluntary Organisations for the Handicapped
29, Eaton Sq, Monkstown, Co. Dublin
Tel: (01) 809251

National umbrella organisation for over forty voluntary organisations who provide services to people with physical and sensory disabilities, and a mental handicap.

Motor Neuron Disease

Motor Neuron Disease
Carmichael House, Nth Brunswick St, Dublin 7
Tel: (01) 721233

Aims to help patients and their families with counselling and funding where necessary. Advice on disease and social welfare problems. Provides aids needed — as decided by community occupational therapists.

Muggings

Victims of Muggins
Referral through local doctor to:
Dr McCormack, Eastern Health Board, 9 Ushers Island, Dublin 8
Tel: (01) 776946

Multiple Sclerosis

Multiple Sclerosis Society of Ireland
2, Sandymount Green, Dublin 4
Tel: (01) 694599

Helps people with MS to help themselves. Provides welfare services and promotes research projects. Runs a trained counselling service, and telephone support and information service.
Regional offices in: Sligo (071) 43089, Cork (021) 300001, Galway (091) 62737, Donegal (074) 25017, Limerick (061) 314111.

Muscular Dystrophy

Muscular Dystrophy
Carmichael House, Nth Brunswick St, Dublin 7
Tel: (01) 721233

Provides information and support to sufferers and their families.

N

Narcotics (See *Drugs*)

O

Ombudsman

Ombudsman
52, St Stephen's Green, Dublin 2
Tel: (01) 785222

The ombudsman investigates complaints from members of the public who feel they have been unfairly treated by bodies such as government departments, local authorities, health boards, Telecom Éireann and An Post. The service is free. Efforts should be made in the first instance to sort out the difficulty with the relevant body.

One-Parent Family (See *Single Parent* and *Pregnancy/Maternity*)

P

Parents Alone

Parents Alone Resource Centre
325, Bunratty Rd, Coolock, Dublin 5
Tel: (01) 481872

Drop-in centre. Support, advice and information for those parenting alone, in the following areas: social welfare, legal or housing issues, personal advice and counselling, child-minding facilities with advice and support in child development. Support groups in personal development. Literacy, home-making and DIY skills. Self-defence classes.

Parents Under Stress

Parents Under Stress
Carmichael House, Nth Brunswick St, Dublin 7
Tel: (01) 733500
A confidential telephone listening service for parents.

Parkinson's Disease

Parkinson's Association of Ireland
Carmichael House, Nth Brunswick St, Dublin 7
Tel: (01) 721233

Aims to support and comfort sufferers of Parkinson's Disease and their relatives; to collect and disseminate information on the disease and to fund research.

Pensioners (Also see *Elderly* and *Retirement*)

Alone
3, Canal Terrace, Bluebell, Dublin 12
Tel: (01) 509614

Aims to promote awareness of old people's problems, rescue those in need, visit and provide them with necessities of life. Refers cases to the task force on special housing aid for the elderly, and monitors same.

Care
Carmichael House, Nth Brunswick St, Dublin 7
Tel: (01) 721233

Aims to provide necessities of life and additional comforts to needy aged living alone. Visits, food, fuel, clothes, bedclothes. A speciality of CARE is to seek out and care for aged people living in bad conditions.

Dublin Central Mission — Social Aid Centre
7, Marlborough Place, Dublin 1
Tel: (01) 742123
Offers care, understanding and advice, and accommodation for the elderly.

Phobias (See *Counselling* and *Family Therapy*)

Physical Handicap

The Department of Education, Marlborough Street, Dublin, will provide information about special schools and classes.

Caring and Sharing Association (CASA)
Carmichael House, Nth Brunswick St, Dublin 7
Tel: (01) 725300/725370

This is an organisation of voluntary helpers and handicapped people. It aims to develop an awareness of the needs of all its members, spiritual, social and personal. It organises socials, bus outings, holiday centres in Ireland, and has an annual pilgrimage to Lourdes and Knock.

Central Remedial Clinic
Penny Ansley Building, Vernon Ave, Clontarf, Dublin 3
Tel: (01) 332206

National medical rehabilitation centre providing a wide range of specialist services on a non-residential basis, with particular emphasis on the management of the child with multiple handicaps. It has fully equipped departments of physiotherapy, occupational therapy, speech therapy, social services and micro-electronics. Specialised treatment and instruction in home management are provided for parents of children with spina bifida, muscular dystrophy and similar physical disabilities. The CRC has a large primary school and pre-school nursery, as well as an adult education service for workshop employees. A day-centre provides occupational and social activation for handicapped adults.

Cerebral Palsy Ireland
Sandymount Ave, Dublin 4
Tel: (01) 695355

This voluntary organisation caters for the physical, educational and medical needs of people with cerebral palsy and other physical disabilities. It operates clinics, schools and workshops in Dublin, Cork, Bray and Kilkenny, and has a branch in nearly every county in Ireland.

Irish Wheelchair Association
Aras Chúchulain, Blackheath Drive, Clontarf, Dublin 3
Tel: (01) 338241/2/3

Established to achieve complete social and economic integration and rehabilitation of wheelchair users. Nationwide network of branches. Provides a range of services including social workers, occupational therapists, youth officers, driving school for the disabled, wheelchair-repair service, transport fleet, facilities for sports, provision of day-care activities and home-care attendant scheme.

National Rehabilitation Board
Clyde Road, Ballsbridge, Dublin 4

Has various information leaflets on different aspects of services available, particularly those relating to training and employment.

Parent to Parent
Carmichael Centre for Voluntary Groups, Nth Brunswick St, Dublin 7
Tel: (01) 724111 (Tuesdays 8 – 10pm)

Support group for parents who have children with physical and/or mental handicap.

Polio Fellowship of Ireland
Vocational Residential Training Centre
Stillorgan Grove, Stillorgan, Co. Dublin
Tel: (01) 888366/833481

This organisation is devoted to the after-care of post-polio and disabled persons. It provides employment for disabled people in its offices, shoe-repair workshop and sheltered packing division.

Vocational training courses for all disabled persons are conducted in the fields of horticulture, catering and food service, bakery and confectionery, accommodation services and laundry.

Rehabilitation Institute
Roslyn Park, Sandymount, Dublin 4
Tel: (01) 698422

This is the major national voluntary organisation in the vocational rehabilitation field. Its objective is to provide vocational training facilities and community workshops for handicapped people. Training and employment facilities are provided for people with physical or mental disabilities in workshops throughout Ireland.

Services are available to all such persons who are assessed as suitable for entry to the training centres or community workshops.

Additional services include remedial education, hostel accommodation, social clubs and residential centres.

Union of Voluntary Organisations of the Handicapped
29 Eaton Sq, Monkstown, Co. Dublin
Tel: (01) 809251/803142

The overall group representing all handicapped organisations. Forty organisations are affiliated, and are involved in the provision of services for people with disabling conditions. A helpful information pack is available on all services.

For details of services locally, contact local Health Board.

Playgroups/Pre-School

Barnardo's
244/246 Harolds' Cross Rd, Dublin 6W
Tel: (01) 977276/977313

Provides and develops in consultation with statutory and other agencies selected services for children and young people in need and for their families. Day foster-care and day nursery in Dun Laoghaire. Community projects and day nurseries in Tallaght, Mulhuddart, Blanchardstown and Ballybrack. Community project in Fatima Mansions.

Irish Pre-School Playgroups Association
19, Wicklow St, Dublin 2
Tel: (01) 719245

Promotes the formation of playgroups in Ireland. Aims to increase public awareness of the needs of pre-school children and their parents. Provides advisory and back-up services to parents and play-leaders. Voluntary registration of playgroups.

Irish Society for the Prevention of Cruelty to Children (ISPCC)
20 Molesworth St, Dublin 2
Tel: (01) 760423/4/5

Provides a variety of family support services. Family centres, therapeutic pre-schools and community workers nationwide.

World Organisation for Early Childhood Education (OMEP)
c/o ISPCC, 20 Molesworth St, Dublin 2
Tel: (01) 6793333

Aims to promote the care/education of young children and to stimulate public interest in servicing their needs. Provides meeting-place for members and groups to discuss children's issues.

Pre-Menstrual Tension (See *Family Planning*)

Pregnancy/Maternity (Also see *Unmarried Parent* and *Single Parent*)

Born Before their Time
48 Wyvern, Killiney, Co Dublin
Tel: (01) 350085

Support group for parents who have premature babies.

Caesarean Support Group
14, Vernon Grove, Rathgar, Dublin 6
Tel: (01) 971762

Aims to provide information and support on caesarean section.

Cherish
2 Lower Pembroke St, Dublin 2
Mon to Fri, 10am – 1pm, 2.15 – 5.30pm
Tel: (01) 682744

This non-denominational organisation provides a free and confidential service for single women during and after pregnancy, with emphasis on self-help and mutual support.
Services provided include information and advice to personal callers, and by letter and telephone; counselling service and advice on social welfare allowances, taxation, legal aspects, medical services, day care, retraining and employment opportunities.
Also practical help, such as second-hand cots, prams, baby clothes, and limited short-term accommodation.
Group meetings for single parents and pregnant women are held on the first Thursday of every month.

Cura
30 South Anne St, Dublin 2
Tel: (01) 710598

Established by the Catholic bishops, this organisation aims to provide counselling and practical help for girls and women with unplanned pregnancies. There is a confidential phone service at the following numbers: Dublin (01) 710598; Kilkenny (056) 22739; Cork (021) 501444; Waterford (051) 76452; Limerick (061) 48207; Galway (091) 7077; Sligo (071) 3659; Derry (08-050-4) 268467; Belfast (084) 644963; Ennis (065) 29905; Wexford (053) 22255; Athlone (0902) 74272; Dundalk (042) 37533.

Cura can arrange pregnancy tests, post-abortion counselling, accommodation in private homes or in mother and baby homes. Advice on financial and legal matters, some financial aid. Short-term foster care for approx. six weeks after the birth of the baby. They also arrange referrals to adoption agencies, and post-adoption counselling.

Federation of Services for Unmarried Parents and their Children
36 Upper Rathmines Rd, Dublin 6
Tel: (01) 964155

This body is an umbrella organisation representing the many bodies working in the area of unmarried parents. It deals with the many areas which may be of concern to the single mother or father, such as medical care, maternity leave, where to stay during pregnancy, social welfare benefits, adoption, foster care, the legal rights and responsibilities of the father, and the status and rights of the child.

Home Birth Centre of Ireland
The Mews, 4 Leinster Rd, Dublin 6
Tel: (01) 977342

Aims to present home birth as an option and to work in the long-term for the reintegration of home birth into the general medical services. Group meetings in Dublin for prospective parents.

Irish Stillbirth and Neonatal Death Society
P.O. Box 2475, Swords, Co. Dublin
Tel: (01) 859791/809163/831919

Group of parents who have experienced the loss of a baby around the time of birth, and are willing to befriend and support other bereaved families.

Irish Sudden Infant Death Association
Carmichael House, Nth Brunswick St, Dublin 7
Tel: (01) 747007

Aims to help and support parents bereaved by sudden infant death (cot death) and to raise funds for research. Organises meetings, seminars, disseminates information, etc. 24-hour telephone help-line. Befriending service, and drop-in centre for bereaved families.

La Leche League
P.O. Box 1280, Raheny, Dublin 5
Tel: (01) 463248

International organisation which helps mothers who want to breast-feed their babies. Local groups and individual counsellors (see Telephone Directories) offer information, leaflets, books, and informal gatherings for mothers.

Life
29/30 Dame St, Dublin 2
Tel: (01) 798989
77, Grand Parade, Cork
Tel: (021) 270445
Little Flower Hall, Bray, Co. Wicklow
Tel: (01) 863975

Provides a caring service for women with unplanned pregnancies. Counselling and pregnancy testing service is available. Short-term accommodation for single pregnant girls and mothers with babies is arranged.

Miscarriage Association of Ireland
27 Kenilworth Rd, Dublin 6
Tel: (01) 972938

Aims to provide support and information following miscarriage.

Pact
71, Brighton Rd, Dublin 6
Tel: (01) 906438

Provides an inter-denominational counselling service for unmarried parents to enable them to come to a considered decision about their own and their child's future. Help is given to obtain medical care, accommodation, financial support, employment, and day care. An adoption placement service is also available.

Post-Natal Depression Support Group
2, Dara Crescent, Celbridge, Co. Kildare

Prisoners

Allowances for Prisoners' Wives
Tel: (071) 69800; (01) 748444

Application forms can be obtained from the local social welfare offices, or from Pension Services Office, Dept of Social Welfare,
College Rd, Sligo.

Dublin Central Mission (Social Aid Centre)
7, Marlborough Place, Dublin 1
Tel: (01) 742123

Offers care, understanding, advice and rehabilitation for ex-prisoners. Friendship centre. Coffee bar. Second-hand clothes shop.

Irish Commission for Prisoners Overseas
Sub-section of Bishops' Commission for Emigrants
7/8 Lr Abbey St, Dublin 1
Tel: (01) 786482/788187, ext. 266

LONDON: Fr. Patrick Smyth, 1 Berrymead Gardens, London W3 8AA
Tel: London 993-9823

Identifies and responds to the needs of Irish prisoners overseas and their families. Researches and provides relevant information to prisoners and groups caring for their welfare.

PACT (Prisoners' Aid Through Community Effort)
7 Upr Leeson St (office).
Tel: (01) 602870)
Priorswood House, Coolock (Hostel)
Santry Hall Industrial Estate, Santry (Workshop)

Involved in the rehabilitation of ex-offenders by providing accommodation, support and encouragement at hostel. Woodwork, metalwork, social skills and literacy training at workshop.

Prisoners' Rights Organisation
35 Lr Buckingham St, Dublin 1
Tel: (01) 365698
75, Lr Sean McDermott St, Dublin 1
Tel: 971003

Aims to reform the prison system, to inform the public about the system, to encourage the rehabilitation of prisoners and the provision of vocational training and constructive after-care. Holds weekly meetings and advice sessions (Tuesdays 7.30 pm), open to everyone, but ex-prisoners and their relatives especially welcome.

Psychologist

Galway Psychological Services
Ruxton House, 35/37 Dominick St, Galway
Tel: (091) 64995

Offers a wide range of services, for children, adolescents and adults. Complete psychological and educational assessment, learning programmes, behaviour programmes, child management strategies, stress management, counselling. Special referral is not required.

Psychologist: Department of Education
Tel: (01) 734700

Psychologists are assigned to secondary schools through the Dept of Education. Contact is usually made through the schools via the careers guidance counsellor. Parents can ring the Department direct for assistance. This service should be available soon to primary schools.

R

Rape (See also *Sexual Assault*)

Rape Crisis Centre
Dublin: 70 Lr Leeson St, Dublin 2
Tel: (01) 614911
Cork: 27A Mac Curtain St, Cork
Tel: (012) 968086

Provides a support system for those who have been raped, sexually assaulted
or are victims of child sexual abuse or incest. Provides individual and group
counselling, both long- and short-term. 24-hour counselling service.
Counsellors from the Centre will accompany clients to court and will arrange
for legal information and advice.

Retirement (See also *Pensioners* and *Elderly*)

Federation of Active Retirement Associations
c/o Retirement Information Centre, 68/71 Gt Strand St, Dublin 1
Tel: (01) 727666

Retirement Planning Council of Ireland
16, Harcourt St, Dublin 2
Tel: (01) 783600

Non-profit, educational body, helps people prepare for retirement. It
organises two-day Planning for Retirement courses, both in-company and
for the general public. It co-operates with Health Boards, VECs etc in
planning community-based courses.

S

Schizophrenia

Schizophrenia Association of Ireland
4, Fitzwilliam Place, Dublin 2
Tel: (01) 761988

Offers a confidential and information service, structured system of support,
guidance and mutual help for sufferers and their families. Local support
groups and branches.

Separation

Aim Group for Family Law Reform
64, Lower Mount St, Dublin 2
Tel: (01) 616478

Campaigns for family law reform, operates a legal information and referral
centre for people with marriage and family problems, and a mediation service
for couples wishing to separate.

Divorce Action Group
P.O. Box 2384, Dublin 6
Tel: (01) 504267

Help and information available for separated persons. Campaigns for the removal of the constitutional ban on divorce and on issues relevant to separated persons.

Family Mediation Service
Irish Life Centre, Block 1, Floor 5, Lr. Abbey St, Dublin 1
Tel: (01) 728277

A professional, free and confidential service under the auspices of the Dept of Justice, to help couples who have decided to separate, to negotiate with the minimum of distress or bitterness their own separation terms on any or all of the following: ongoing parenting of the children; maintenance; family home and property. This is *not* a marriage counselling or legal advice centre.

Separated Persons Association
Carmichael House, Nth Brunswick St, Dublin 7
Tel: (01) 721233

Aims to give encouragement to those whose marriages have broken down. Advocates law reform in the area of marriage breakdown. Holds meetings, social events. Branch in Cork.

Sexual Assault/Abuse

Child-Line Freephone
c/o ISPCC
Tel: (01) 6793333

COUNSELLORS IN PRIVATE PRACTICE:

Rosemary Liddy, Bernie Purcell, Michelle O'Sullivan
(ex. Rape Crisis Centre Staff)
Roebuck House
Tel: (01) 838792

Imelda McCarthy (Family therapist in The Mater and UCD)
The Vico Centre, Dun Laoghaire
Tel: (01) 843336

Marie Keenan
55, Ranelagh, Dublin 6
Tel: (01) 971188

Dr. Michelle Cahill
(nr Montrose Hotel)
Tel: (01) 693009

Irish Parents Together
c/o 13, Bayview Close, Kilcoole, Co. Wicklow
Tel: (01) 875587

Support group for parents of sexually abused children.

Irish Society for the Prevention of Cruelty to Children
20, Molesworth St, Dublin 2
Tel: (01) 760452/760423/4/5

Rape Crisis Centre Cork
Tel: (021) 968086

Provides a support system for victims of rape/sexual assault or incest. Group and individual counselling. Telephone counsellors. Complete confidentiality.

Rape Crisis Centre Dublin
70, Lr Leeson St, Dublin 2
Tel: (01) 614911

TREATMENT UNITS:

Crumlin Hospital, Dublin
Tel: (01) 558220/558221

For children from the Southside of Dublin and other regions.

Rotunda Hospital, Dublin 1
Tel: (01) 730700

For teenagers and adults. Validation of sexual abuse. Initial treatment, and referral to appropriate agency.

Temple Street Hospital, Dublin 2
Tel: (01) 745214/742887

For children from the Northside of Dublin.

Sexually Transmitted Diseases

Clinics:
Mater Hospital, Dublin (01) 304488.
Regional Hospital, Dooradoyle, Limerick (061) 28111.
Regional Hospital, Ardkeen, Waterford (051) 73321.
St James's Hospital, Dublin (01) 535245/537941.
Victoria Hospital, Cork (021) 966844.

In Galway there is a confidential telephone line (091) 64000.

Single Parent (Also see *Unmarried Parent* and *Pregnancy*)

Challenge
Sion House, Sion Rd, Kilkenny
Tel: (056) 21653/61210

Provides counselling and support services for single parents and their families.

Cherish
2, Lr Pembroke St, Dublin 2
Tel: (01) 682744

Group meetings for single parents held monthly. Practical help available such as cots, prams etc. Advice and counselling.

Gingerbread
Top floor, 12, Wicklow St, Dublin 2
Tel: (01) 710291

A self-help organisation for one-parent families. Provides encouragement and guidance to bring about change in matters relating to one-parent families. The association runs branch meetings, teenage group social activities, group holidays for parents and children. There is a legal advice clinic, counselling and mediation — all free of charge. Branches throughout the country.

Society of St Vincent de Paul

Headquarters
Cabra Rd, Dublin 7
Tel: (01) 384164/384167

Practical help available. Child-care centre. Holidays arranged. See Telephone Directory for local branches.

Spina Bifida (Also see *Physical Handicap*)

Spina Bifida
Old Nangor Rd, Clondalkin, Dublin 22
Tel: (01) 572326

Care, welfare, treatment, education, advancement and rehabilitation of persons suffering from Spina Bifida. Footwear and Caliper Repair centre. Twelve branches throughout the country.

Stroke

Volunteer Stroke Scheme
249, Crumlin Rd, Dublin 12
Tel: (01) 557455
Aims to help patients recovering from stroke, particularly in the area of communication. Arranges home visits. Phone for local schemes.

Sudden Infant Death (See *Cot Death*)

Suicide

The Samaritans
112, Marlborough St, Dublin 1
Tel: (01) 727700
Works for the prevention of suicide, and befriends the lonely, despairing and suicidal.

T

Teenagers (See *Adolescent*)

Transvestism

Friends of Eon
c/o Irish Family Planning Assoc, 15 Mountjoy Sq, Dublin 1
Tel: (01) 740723
Counselling service available. Phone for times of service.

Transvestite Group
c/o Hirschfield Centre, Fownes St, Dublin 2
Tel: (01) 710939
Transvestite-support telephone line.

U

Unemployed

Dolebusters' Unemployment Resource Centre
18a Adelaide Rd, Dublin 2
Tel: (01) 619670

Helps people prepare for interviews and provides job information and encouragement.

Irish National Organisation of the Unemployed
48, Fleet St, Dublin 2
Tel: (01) 795316

All-Ireland federation of unemployed centres and action groups providing support and co-ordination.

Unmarried Parent (Also see *Pregnancy/Maternity* and *Single Parent*)

Challenge
Sion House, Sion Rd, Kilkenny
Tel: (056) 21653/61210

Provides counselling and support services for single parents and their families. Promotes community awareness and involvement in this area. Provides pregnancy testing, ante-natal accommodation and medical care. Counselling for pre- and post-natal stages. Foster-care for limited period. Adoption arranged. Help with day-care. Befriending service for women keeping their babies. Also a registered adoption society. Post-adoption counselling service and post-abortion counselling available.

Federation of Services for Unmarried Parents and their Children
36, Upper Rathmines Rd, Dublin 6
Tel: (01) 964155

National non-denominational body. Provides information and referral service for clients at pre- and post-natal stages. Aims to co-ordinate all services and research in the area of unmarried parenthood.

Shelter Referral
Ballyogan House, Ballyogan Rd, Carrickmines, Dublin 18
Tel: (01) 955969

Provides residential accommodation for up to ten expectant unmarried mothers.

St Patrick's Guild
Mother and Child Welfare Agency and Adoption Service
82, Haddington Rd, Dublin 4
Tel: (01) 681765/691908

Aims to provide information, practical help and counselling for any mother — unmarried or married. Also fathers, children, parents and anyone who needs help. Confidential counselling, free pregnancy testing, accommodation in Mother and Baby homes, hospitals, or with families. Temporary care and help towards permanent care of child; adoption placement if required; post-adoption counselling for adopters and adoptees.

V

Visually Impaired (See *Blind*)

W

Well Woman Centre (See *Family Planning*)

Women's Aid (See *Homeless*)

Y

Youth

Acted
Carmichael Centre for Voluntary Groups, Nth Brunswick St, Dublin 7

To recruit as members all those involved in working with young people and adults in the community, outside of formal schooling situations.

Catholic Youth Council
20/23, Arran Quay, Dublin 7
Tel: (01) 725055

Supports and promotes youth work and youth ministry in the archdiocese
of Dublin by providing training, education, competitions, residential centres
and information. Enquiries here as to what's available in each locality.

Church of Ireland Youth Council
74, Upr Leeson St, Dublin 2
Tel: (01) 607122

Co-ordinates youth work and the provision of services and resources through
a network of area youth councils. Provides training for youth leaders along
with events and opportunities for developing young people.

Cork Youth Enquiry Service
YMCA, 11/12 Marlboro St, Cork
Tel: (021) 273056/270187

Information and resource centre for young people and those concerned with
needs of youth.

EC Schemes for Young People
Details from FÁS, Higher Education Authority, and the Irish Office of the
EC, Jean Monnet House, Molesworth St, Dublin 2. (Tel: 01-712244)

National Council of YMCAs of Ireland Ltd
St George's Buildings, 37/41, High St, Belfast 1
Tel: (01) 327757

Aims to provide physical, social, educational and spiritual activities for young
people, to help them develop their lives and be of service to others.

National Youth Council of Ireland
3, Montague St (off Hatch St) Dublin 2
Tel: (01) 784122

Coordinating body for voluntary youth organisations, representing over
half a million young people in Ireland. Works on behalf of youth
organisations to promote the development of services for young people.
NYCI is the coordinating and monitoring body for youth information.

No Name Club
Tel: (01) 212172

Aims to provide a positive alternative to 'pub culture'.

Youth Exchange Bureau
10, Lower Hatch St, Dublin 2
Tel: (01) 618738

Aims to promote and develop exchange opportunities for young Irish people.

Youth Information Centre
Sackville Place, Dublin 2 (By side of Clerys)

Provides information on holiday/work schemes, etc.

Youth Training Programmes
For information contact the local FÁS Office.

Index